THE HOLISTIC ENTREPRENEUR

CREATING SUCCESS WITH THE MEDICINE OF YOUR SOUL

NADINE ROBINSON

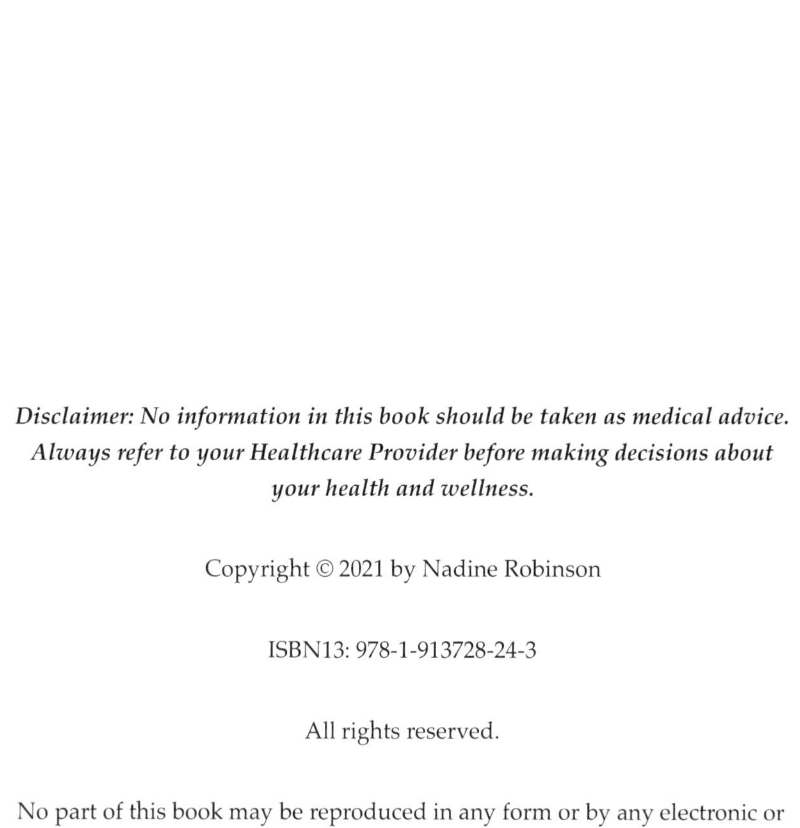

Disclaimer: No information in this book should be taken as medical advice. Always refer to your Healthcare Provider before making decisions about your health and wellness.

ISBN13: 978-1-913728-24-3

CONTENTS

INTRODUCTION

I am so glad you have picked up this book. You are about to embark on a journey that will challenge you, scare you, inspire you and help you manifest your life filled with happiness and success.

If you have never heard the term "Holistic Entrepreneur", that's cool; a lot of people haven't heard of it. And you're in the right place. Holistic entrepreneurs are those amazing people who have a great idea or product. They strive for a life in balance while living deeply in integrity and abiding by the principle "win/win or no go". Holistic entrepreneurs commit to serving themselves and their clients. There is no lack mindset, although we all deal with money mindset and confidence blocks at some point. There is no trying to just get the sale. Holistic entrepreneurs truly want to see their clients and customers successful and thriving.

I wrote this book because I have mentored hundreds of people who have incredible skills and creativity. They have a great solution to their client's problems. However, there is a gigantic gap for many of us; how do we build this amazing business? Many of the traditional business books don't address our needs. We are not hardcore, cutthroat businesspeople. We don't want to work 18-hour days, 7 days a week. We want success, but our definition is usually not just a dollar value. We want to get our products and services out to our clients, but we aren't willing to trick them. We won't use high-pressure sales tactics or behave in a way that leaves us, or our clients, feeling like we need a shower after the interaction.

This book will help you bridge the gap between sales, marketing, branding, money blocks and other important business aspects, and merge it with the holistic tools and resources you need to show up in integrity with yourself and your clients. Your business is an extension of your wild heart, innovation and balanced lifestyle. Your clients will love the way you do business.

Close your eyes and imagine your image of success right now. You know what it looks and feels like. This book will get you there while learning even more about yourself along the way.

If you are looking for a quick fix book, I hate to disappoint you, but you are in the wrong place. Holistic entrepreneurship is about a lifestyle and a set of beliefs and values that centres integrity and wholeness as guiding principles and weaves them throughout the fabric of your life.

I have been a holistic entrepreneur my entire life. This is my 4th business start-up. I started a successful Doula and Childbirth Education business when I was 22 years old. I started a midwifery practice with over 10 midwives, staff and managed budgets of well over $2,000,000.00 a year. My husband and I own and run, with 2 other amazing partners, a successful company and finally, I am here, owner and creatrix at Peace Healing Wellness, providing people with the holistic and energetic tools to live the life of their dreams.

Make sure you dive into this book and see how you feel. As a holistic entrepreneur, I want you to finish reading this book feeling hopeful, empowered and knowing the next steps you need to take to create your successful business.

If you are looking for sustained growth and success with a holistic lens, then you've got one of the best and most unique resources in the world, right here at your fingertips. Dive in, have fun, and learn even more about who you are and how you can truly live your life on fire.

Big WILD love to you.

xo

Nadine

How to use this book:

This is not a book that you sit back and read. Grab and journal and a pen. Be prepared to be stretched. You will be uncomfortable. There might be things you dislike. This is the good stuff. Write down your thoughts as you move through the book. What do you agree with? What do you strongly disagree with?

When you see the header HOT TIP, take a few moments to follow the exercise described there. These are potent teaching moments that will help you clarify your why and offer you tips and techniques to get the results you are looking for.

1

WHAT IS A HOLISTIC ENTREPRENEUR?

Holistic Entrepreneurs are those amazing humans who have not only created or want to start a business, but they are also absolutely committed to integrity, see themselves as being in service to their clients and want a balanced and healthy lifestyle.

Entrepreneurship can be hard. This the 4th successful business that I have started. Each one had its own unique challenges and opportunities. As a holistic entrepreneur, you are not just concerned with the sale, money, and getting ahead. Being kind, offering real solutions, bringing joy to your clients and truly finding that space of balance, happiness and joy in your life are key.

Holistic Entrepreneurs really live the mantra "Treat others how you would like to be treated."

Hot Tip: *Take a moment here to jot down what your mantra is as it relates to your business.*

Seeking success, financially, personally, within your business and in all other areas in your life are not dichotomous. The minute you start to take the time to balance and create the successful life you want in one area of your life, that energy has no other choice but to flow into all the rest of your areas of your world.

Holistic entrepreneurs are different. We ache if we get out of alignment. We are willing to put in the time and effort to shift out of negative cultural beliefs of "hard work = success" or other damaging narratives. Holistic entrepreneurs are willing to be challenged in their thinking, their offerings and their beliefs. We allow ourselves to be influenced by the ideas and wisdom of others. We know constructive criticism is a strength and allows us to expand our reality. When we understand how other people might be thinking and feeling, we can tailor our offerings to even better serve our clients. Holistic entrepreneurs are perennial students. We read, take courses, and pick ourselves up when we make mistakes because we are always learning.

Holistic entrepreneurs are able to react and respond to failures, flops, mistakes, errors and missteps. We might stubbornly hold onto our vision and hold it tight, and yet we are not afraid to learn from our mistakes and pivot.

Holistic entrepreneurs know that their businesses are an extension of themselves. This is reflected in mindset, confidence, how we serve our clients, what types of offerings we have and a whole host of other things. This can also be extremely difficult because we can easily take things personally and failure can feel like a personal flaw. Would you like to know how to be in alignment with your business and also have the resilience to carry on even when things are tough or challenging?

Hot Tip: *Set your timer on your phone for 1 minute. Brainstorm every belief you have that relates to success, work and money. Let your pen fly across the page and see what shows up for you.*

Lifestyle is a huge part of holistic entrepreneurship, whether that'sbeing able to go camping for a week, skiing in the winter, travelling while still earning money. Maybe you want to live in a van. Holistic entrepreneurs can be a little weird. We are constantly evaluating how to create the life we want and making micro-tweaks to ensure it's exactly what we are dreaming of. If you are new to holistic entrepreneurship you might be wondering "how can I have the lifestyle I want and start a new successful business?" Don't worry. I have some fascinating tools in this book that will help you to create your amazing life too.

Finally, an important differentiation on relationships. If you have ever read anything about marketing or other books about business, I am sure you have heard, "People buy from people". Holistic entrepreneurs take this to the next level. Not only will you be super intimate with your ideal client, you actually want them to be happy, empowered and joyful when they are working with you.

Now, that's not to say you won't disappoint people, have people be angry with you or mess up. I guarantee you will. And it will hurt you heart. And that's good. This book is going to help you leverage that as motivation, rather than get stuck in being down in the dumps and taking that criticism and those failures to heart.

Personal relationships are also very important to holistic entrepreneurs. They want to love and have time to spend with their family. They want a wild and horny sex life. They want good, deep and nourishing friendships. They want to love themselves, their body, and feel that deep joy within from meaningful connection.

Holistic entrepreneurship is not just for one or two industries. It's not just for healers, wellness practitioners, massage therapists, naturopaths, doulas or anyone else in the health and wellness business. It's for painters, coffee shop owners, hardware stores, and your local florist.

If you want to have a beautiful life and provide a great service or product to your client, you are a holistic entrepreneur.

Sound ambitious? A little pie in the sky for you? Are you thinking "no way can anyone have it all"? Then you are in the right place.

You can have it all. It will look different for you than for me. That's the whole point. This book will help you embrace your amazing gifts and talents, get you clear on what you want and what it looks like and feels like, and will give you real strategies to manifest that life and sustain it.

A Quick Note if you are in the Healing or Wellness Industry.

Stepping into the role of a healer is a dichotomy. All healers know that all beings are deserving of healing. This is why holistic entrepreneurship is a cornerstone to most healing practices. The relationship with running a business and offering healing can be very difficult to navigate for many healers.

This book is written with you in mind. I will furnish you with the best tools to find that sweet spot of offering your services, aligned and in accordance with your highest good and the highest good of the people you are serving.

So many great healers' burnout, or are doing their practice as a side gig because they cannot afford their lives due to the pittance they are charging.

Take the time to go through this book. Reflect deeply on your relationship to healing and the business of it. Honour your own knowing and beliefs here. And most importantly, I want to challenge you to get creative and offer your services in a dynamic and fresh way. It's not business or healing. Remember, it's win/win or no go. Hold that in the forefront of your brain as we go on this healing journey of self-discovery. What will you find?

2

WHAT'S YOUR WHY?

This is probably one of the most important pieces of the puzzle for holistic entrepreneurs. Why do you get up in the morning? What makes the hard work and long hours' worth it? How are you serving your clients?

Until you know your why, you will be caught in the agitation of hustle, flip flop, work hard and repeat without the prosperity and gratification that your business can bring you.

If you are an entrepreneur, I know you are hard working. Your confidence is probably pretty good. You're not afraid to try something and fail. That is going to keep you in your zone of excellence. That sounds pretty good. Sadly, this is where a whole lot of entrepreneurs fail. They stick in their zone of excellence because they are good at what they do and it's fairly easy. These are tasks and skills that you probably had an aptitude for and feel effortless.

Where you really want to be is in your zone of genius. (Check out Gay Hendricks book "The Big Leap" for more on this concept.) Your zone of genius is that special something and the secret sauce that only you can deliver. It's a unique set of skills, experience, wisdom, life journeys, and products and services that only you can share. This is what sets you apart.

Do you know what your core values are? Does your business have core values? Core values help you appreciate what motivates you. This helps you understand your why.

Core values also give us the pathway to our how. It takes a whole lot of guesswork out of our journey and provides clear and direct next steps in your business. You've heard the story that there are lots of ways up to the top of the mountain? Sure. But I don't love climbing mountains, so I want to get dropped off from a helicopter and open a bottle of prosecco. My husband, on the other hand, would be happy to climb for 8 hours, hit the top and open a can of sardines. One isn't better than the other; it's just an outward expression of our core values.

You can catch my video on how to figure out your core values HERE or follow the suggestions below.

https://youtu.be/WsPAFVxwae0

Hot Tip: *Let's do an easy exercise to help you find your core values. Set the timer on your phone for 2 minutes. Write down all* *the words that feel important to you. Try not to judge or evaluate. Just observe the words that feel like they are powerful for you.*

Once you have done that, you can reset your timer for 60 seconds. I now want you to write down what you think are important values that you would want to teach children. Again, don't evaluate, just allow yourself to see what is important.

You now have your core values. You will need to narrow them down to about 3-5 words. Notice which ones are similar. For example, knowledge, wisdom and learning are quite similar. If you choose those words, which one embodies the feeling you want the most? You might want to check out a thesaurus and really hone your choices. In this case the word "curiosity" is what embodies how I value learning and wisdom.

My personal core values are Love, Consideration, Curiosity and Integrity. Once I knew what they were, it made everything easier. As holistic entrepreneurs, we know that our businesses are simply an extension of ourselves, so why not align early and stop working against ourselves? This is especially important when we are evaluating business and marketing strategies. If you are following some recommended formula that is completely unaligned it's never going to be authentic and flow. You know it's not great for you or your clients. It's going to be choppy and bumpy and sticky. You might find some success, but it might be in spite of yourself.

Core values give you your why. It doesn't matter what your industry is, what your skills are or what your business is. Once you know what your core values are, you have the road map that will guide you and help you navigate the wild ride that entrepreneurship is.

Mission, Vision, Core Values and Goals.

Now that you know your own personal core values, it's time to sit down and clarify the purpose of your business.

A lot of entrepreneurs miss this step because there is so much to do. Raising capital, cash flow, suppliers, hiring consultants and staff, market assessment, PR and social media, gaining a client base, business planning and strategy, establishing yourself as the expert... the list goes on. However, at one point you will run into an issue that will cost you time and money. While we cannot control other's behaviours around us, when we know our mission, vision, core values and goals, a lot of the time we can reroute ourselves earlier to get off a collision course.

Many entrepreneurs, because they are extremely creative, think outside the box and see a need, or niche that can be filled, and jump in quickly to get things started. This is a superpower, and it can also hold us back. We may spend loads of time on great ideas that actually don't fill our heart space and make us sing for joy when we get out of bed in the morning. Even if you're good at something, even if it's easy, take the time to get crystal clear on these four basics of your business. They are foundational. They ground you into your purpose and will keep you on track.

Mission:

Your mission is what your business sets out to do. What solution do you offer? What transformation can you help with? What problem do you solve?

The more distinct your mission is, the easier it will be for you to nail down what you want to offer, how you offer it and who your market is.

HOT TIP: *Take a few moments and think of your business as fully operational right now. You are successful. Things are up and running smoothly. Close your eyes. Where are you? Where is your office? Who is around you? Do you have staff? How are you spending most of your day? What's the most satisfying feedback you could hear in your day? How much money are you making in a month? How much money are you making in a year? Write all this down in your journal.*

My Mission: *To help wild women know themselves better so they can live the life of their dreams.*

Notice there is no "how" in that statement. It is a simple declaration of what I am here on the Earth to do. This is a soul purpose for me. This is my passion.

You will also notice that this mission could also relate to my midwifery career. I was supporting, guiding and creating sacred space for women and families to blossom into one of the most exciting and momentous journeys of their lives. Many of the women and families I served were wild. They were edgy and they thought outside the box. They were wild women.

Here's the key: your mission in life is probably closely related to your soul path. That's your zone of genius. That's where you will be on fire. Even though my midwifery career and Wild Medicine Woman career look very different, they feel the same on the inside. I am passionate, on fire, and unstoppable. Even on the bad days, I feel the thrum in my heart. Welcome to your mission, should you choose to accept it.

Hot Tip: *Take a few moments now and write down in your journal what your mission is. Don't get hung up on the words or perfection of it.*

Your mission will change and evolve as you and your business change and evolve. Put your mission in a place where you will see it every day. It could be on your bathroom mirror or as the screensaver on your phone. Allow yourself to be reminded daily of who you are and why you get up in the morning to serve your clients.

Vision:

Vision is that space of "in a perfect world". This is the dream space. It's the space of intention, equality, and pure love. For a holistic entrepreneur, this space is very different than a regular entrepreneur.

Many entrepreneurs have mastered the art of entrepreneurship to best afford a lifestyle, financial rewards, societal standing and the reputation that they want. They know how to work the system to have the best possible outcome for themselves and, sometimes, their staff. While nothing is wrong with this, I hope you can feel how different this is for holistic entrepreneurs. If your lens is win/win or no go, then you know that the success of you and your business will directly benefit the success of your family, your friends and your community. That's the results we want to see. Success for ourselves and others.

I once saw a post on social media from someone who is quite wealthy and famous. It was alluding to the idea that they are happy to buy the private jet because it means that other people get jobs. Capitalism at its best; I consume and therefore contribute to the overall health and wellbeing of the economy and others. Someone smarter than me posted a response (and I'm paraphrasing) "Well, this is assuming the people building the jet are paid a good, living wage, have excellent working conditions, proper health and wellness benefits and lots of vacation time."

That's how holistic entrepreneurs work. That's how we see the world. It's not dog eat dog. We will find a solution that works for everyone, including the planet. Then we all succeed.

Ok, I'm off the soapbox. But not really. What's your perfect world? If everyone you served with your mission was "there", what would that feel like? How would things be different and better? What solution are you providing to the world?

Don't diminish yourself. Dream a little. How are you going to dent the universe? (that's an early Steve Jobs quote). Your work matters. How are you helping the community? What knowing and experience do you have that can really help how people go about their lives?

Maybe you own a paving company. Have you heard the complaints about potholes? I live in cold and wintery Canada where salt, snow and gravel are dumped on our roads for 8 months of the year. The roads really take a beating. Thank you paving companies for less wear and tear on my car, making sure I don't dump hot coffee in my lap when I hit a pothole and making our cities safer. This service changes my life.

My Vision: That every woman has the confidence, resources and resiliency to create and sustain a life that is empowering, nourishing and fulfilling.

Sound a little pie in the sky? Yeah, I think so too. There are a lot of problems and issues in the world that I don't think I will see healed and resolved in my lifetime. That's ok. I am still willing to hold that vision. I am willing to see it so firmly and strongly in my mind's eye that each and every decision I make is laser focused on helping to create this world. I trust you will do that too.

Hot Tip: *Take a minute now and write down your vision. Don't get caught up on getting it right. If everyone on the planet had the outcome and solutions that your business was offering (your mission), what would the world look like? What would be amazing and better and fabulous and easy and how would there be more love and happiness in the world?*

Just take a quick stab at this. Again, it will evolve and grow as you start to realize who you are and how you want to, and can best, serve your clients.

Write your vision down now with your core values and your mission. Keep all three present and visually engaging so you can be reminded of why you get up in the morning.

Core Values:

We already talked a bit about core values for you personally. You also need core values for your business.

Your business will have an energy and cadence all its own. It's important to take the time to flesh out the core values for your business. They might be slightly different and, in fact, it's a real bonus if you envision your business as an entity all its own. This will give you some perspective and also help you to minimize internalizing those losses and failures as personal. It's a helpful step to help you build the resiliency you need to ensure you can respond and rebound from missteps and mistakes.

To do the core values exercise for your business, do them first by yourself. Even if you have staff, partners, investors or other people who are involved in your business, take the time to do this exercise by yourself.

Hot Tip: *Go back up and review the Core Values exercise. Write down your Mission and Values statements. Feel into the energy and really focus on how you are here to serve. Then repeat the core values exercise for your business. Take your time to flow through this and get it right. Use a thesaurus and map out associate and supportive words. Take the time to get this smooth and let it be a dynamic reflection of what's important to your business.*

Write down your core values and their supporting and associate words, and place them in a space where you will see them, along with your mission and vision. Access and leverage these foundational pieces when making business decisions, creating new products or content, or perhaps when deciding how to respond to an unhappy client.

Your businesses core values now give you a framework for many other steps and processes in your business that I bet you didn't think of:

- You now have an interview framework and set of questions to ensure the people you are hiring are a good fit, and not just because they have a snazzy resume;
- You know what type of suppliers, accountants and other consultants your business will want to seek out;

- Your strategic plan will now meet the litmus test of your mission, vision, and core values;
- Your operations, processes and systems will flow from your core values;
- Your core values will inform how you run your cashflow;
- Raising capital is now a partnership that blossoms between yourself and your investors;
- Your marketing and social media strategy will align with your core values;
- You can more easily identify your ideal client;
- You will eliminate a whole bunch of options and ideas because they don't match your core values and you will more quickly niche down into your zone of genius;
- Benefits, vacations, salary, and bonuses will root deeply in the foundation of your core values.

Once you have done the core values exercise for your business, it's important to get your business partner to do the same, if you have one. Then you will need to brainstorm and work together to ensure you have captured exactly what each of you imagines what the core values are for your business enterprise.

Once you complete the core values for your business, I would encourage you to have a meeting with any staff or regular contractors you might have. You can share your core values with them and ask them for feedback. This type of openness allows you to build trust within the company and also builds in a safety net.

We are all going to stray and start down a path, create a solution or an offering that just might not resonate enough with your mission, vision and core values. And sometimes we might not see it. Does that ever happen to you? You are so sure of something but it's a total flop? Recognize how wise and knowing your contractors, employees, staff and business partners can be. Because when they know the values of the company, someone can speak up and offer their opinion. Whether or not your listen to that feedback is a whole other chapter, however, this framework will support you to stay true to your path and allow you one more opportunity to stay in your zone of genius.

Peace Healing Wellness' Core Values: Integrity, Love, Curiosity, Self-Knowledge.

Three of my personal core values have also shown up in my business core values. The one difference, consideration as a personal core value and self-knowledge as a business core value, is critical. A huge part of my business is trusting that people know themselves. They know what they need. This is a foundational piece that offers respect and autonomy to my clients. The only way I can serve them is if I recognize them for the expert in their life that they are. I truly believe that we can be perfect and a work in progress at the same time. Breathe into that for a moment and see how it lands. Hokey? Maybe. But it has served me and the thousands of clients I have helped over the years. And when I hold those ideals up to the light, they shine brightly and allow me to trust the path of each person around me, even when it's hard and painful and sticky.

Goals and goal setting are the final foundational piece to your business. They are also loaded with stereotypes, beliefs and experiences that prevent many people from attaining their goals. Because of theses complexities the whole next chapter is devoted to getting goal setting right and working for you.

Your mission, vision and core values may evolve as your business does. Take the time to explore them and allow them to inform what decisions you make in your business and you will see success that also feels powerfully aligned with who you are.

3

GOAL SETTING AND HOW TO MAKE IT WORK FOR YOU

Your Brain Might Be Tripping You up.

What has your experience up until now been with goal setting? Do you like it? Does it work for you?

Humans are creatures of habit. We love to find our little safe zones and hold onto them. And we can get very grumpy if somebody tries to mess with our system. This is the main reason that we set goals and don't stick with it. It's not that we are lazy or weak. It's that we have a series of habits, micro judgements, beliefs and behaviours that work and are good enough.

Ok, a quick lesson in neurobiology. There is a part of our brain called the reticular activator system (RAS). This is a very cool part of our brain that consists of a bundle of nerves. It's job? To filter information. Now, the amazing thing about our RAS is that it picks out things that are important to us. But how does it decide what's important?

Let's remember that the primary job of our brain is to keep us alive. Its whole purpose is to maintain safety and security, to keep the chemistry balanced, to support our hormones to do their job and maintain homeostasis within the body. Heart beating? Check! Breathing? Perfect. No immediate dangers around us? Amazing. But this doesn't mean we will be happy. It doesn't mean we are fulfilled. It doesn't ensure joy, pleasure, laughter, connection or love. But the brain has done its job. And that's all that matters.

So, how does our RAS decide what to focus on and what's important?

We know from the study of epigenetics that our gene expression can be affected by our ancestor's experiences and surroundings. And let's face it, the reason you're alive is because your ancestors ran faster than someone else and got away from the cave lion. Ergo, you now know that you must run away from cave lions. But what if your ancestors ran east and the people who got eaten ran west? Does that mean that it is only safe to run east to get away from cave lions? Hmmm. You see how we might take information, filter it through our brain and land on a conclusion?

Let's remember, running for your life from a cave lion is scary business. So, not only have we had a big lesson and ancestral memory about ancient safety practices, but we also know that we must run east. This survival memory is anchored in high emotion. Passed down now through the generations is the importance of running east to get away from cave lions. This could impact where the community's home is located. It could impact how close or far this home is from the forest or ocean, the mountains or a water source. No longer does "run east to escape cave lions" become a one-off experience, we have hundreds of years of lore, behaviour and knowledge that reinforces this reality. It has become fact.

So, if you brain is here to keep you alive and your RAS is designed to filter information, you will filter it based on past experiences and events, ancestral knowledge, emotions, habits, social and cultural beliefs and norms. Even if you see someone run west and away from a cave lion and they live to talk about it, you brain may filter it out as a fluke, as lucky, or find some other way to dismiss this finding. Running east is the only way to get away from cave lions.

Your RAS also helps explain that when you think PORSCHE, all you see are Porsches. What you focus on and what your brain has decided is "true" and what is "safe" will become what you allow into your mind. Early beliefs and experiences form the basis of what our brain will categorize as normal. The RAS acts as a filing system, filtering anything out that doesn't align with our memories, experiences, ancestral knowledge, beliefs and lived reality.

This is why so many people miss the good stuff. It's not that you are not paying attention to all the love, gifts, pleasure and happiness in your life. You are not ungrateful. If your

RAS has been programmed a certain way, that's what it will filter in. Anything else that doesn't align will be filtered out as an unnecessary detail.

The good news? We can change the RAS and train it to allow new information in and have a new filing system.

This is where goal setting comes in. We all know the definition of insanity is doing the same thing over and over again and expecting a different result. Well, you could say that a lot of us spend our lives insanely setting goals and failing to achieve them because we do not understand how to program our brain and our behaviours to achieve those successes.

HOT TIP: *Do you write goals? Do you tell others your goals? Write down a time that you met your goal and document how you did that. Write down a time you had a goal, and you did not meet your goal. What happened there? Think of a time when you saw someone around you meet their goals. What did you notice, from the outside looking in, that might have contributed to their success?*

Now, how do you actually set yourself up so you can create a goal and make it happen? Keep reading.

Vision Boards.

Has anyone ever heard of vision boards? This is a fun project where you sit down and take some magazines and cut out what you want for yourself. It could be a beautiful home, a beach vacation or a new set of glasses. It could include more family gatherings or a new baby. Maybe you want more money or more clients. Maybe you want more peace in your life. Anything you want should go on the board.

Sadly, vision boards don't work because we often don't know our why. Vision boards also don't work because they are not anchored in meaning. They pull us towards external manifestations of success without the energy of what nourishes our soul.

Think back to the RAS system. It is filtering out extra information and only allows us to see information that we already know about. It's like a filing cabinet and the only thoughts that can get in are the thoughts that are like the ones already in the file.

You can want something. And you might have some success staying focused on it. If I say blue, you are now thinking of blue and can probably see this colour around you. But how long are you actually going to focus on blue? Sure, it's a nice colour and all, but unless you are constantly holding that into the forefront of your mind (or if it's your favourite colour) you will probably lose interest in the colour blue pretty quickly.

That's why your goal setting fails. That's why vision boards don't work. You can sustain this new focus for a short period of time but will quickly revert to the old ways of thinking and behaving. They old ways worked fine anyway. They got you here, didn't they?

If you realize those old ways don't work for you anymore and really want to see some sustained change, then you need to create a new pathway of focus in your brain and new habits so that you can make those changes. You have to provide the RAS with a new opportunity to create that new file, with all the beliefs, behaviours and actions that support this new goal. Small, micro adjustments that you can make daily is what will set you up for success.

Stop dreaming about the car of your dreams. I will show you how to have the car of your dreams.

Embodiment Board.

Instead of making a vision board, I want you to make an embodiment board. An embodiment board is all about feelings. Remember when your ancestor was running away from those cave lions? Not only was the experience a success (I didn't die!) it was also deeply rooted in emotions like fear, elation, relief and a whole whack of other feelings. This is a powerful lesson for you; if you want something different, start to home in on the feeling it will give you.

When creating your embodiment board, do not evaluate or critique what you want. Like a vision board, get really invested in finding photos or symbols that represent what you want. It can be money, clients, better sex, a new car. There should be no limit or judgement on your dreams.

Gather all these images and symbols together and put them on a big piece of paper. Do this really joyfully, knowing that you are now one step closer to creating the life of your dreams. You can use symbols, colours, art, songs, words, poetry or any other creative way of playing here. The more fun and playful and creative you get, the better. This will root deeply in your body. We want to anchor these dreams into reality. Connecting them to your emotions is an easy and successful way to do that.

Let's look at an example. Perhaps you want a big house with a grand, sweeping staircase, large rooms, a huge chef's kitchen, six bedrooms and eight bathrooms. This is great. I love what you are dreaming up here.

But why? What is the feeling behind this house? Having large family gatherings? Hosting dinner parties? Is this house like the house you grew up in? Does this house give you feelings of security? If you could afford a house like that, does that mean you are set, financially, for life? Is this house proof of your success and worth? Don't be afraid to get really vulnerable here. It's ok to want money and power and status. The less judgement you have at this step, the more quickly you will know what's important and what's not.

The emotions I will pull out from this dream house are love, family, community, connection. Fulfillment of childhood memories. Feelings of stability. Feeling worthy. These are all good emotions.

Once you have completed your embodiment board you need to evaluate what the emotions are behind your dreams and wishes. The more connected and clear you can get here, the better. Lean into the story, the longing and the overall messaging that you are trying to create. Don't be afraid to ask for what you want. This is a private exercise just for you. Be honest with yourself. And hey, wouldn't it be fun to not make any of your wishes and dreams wrong?

Whatever the feeling is, write it down. You could even write the feeling underneath the photo or picture you are using to anchor it in. This allows you to deeply connect with the feelings that will help you feel success, happiness, love and abundance you want to create.

Hot Tip: *Give a feeling to every item you want to bring into your life that you put on your embodiment board. If you want a car, write down the feeling that car will give you. If you want a baby, what feelings would that help generate? If you want more money, write down what feeling that money would give you.*

Let's go back to our dream house example. Now that you know that you want love and connection to family, you can start making small changes that will give you those feelings, today. This is how the embodiment board works.

Manifestation is about making it happen right now. When you start generating those feelings, the universe will answer. Your RAS will seek out those feelings because you are making tiny steps to make that your priority. You are saying to your brain "let's focus here." It's not just about the outward things that create the success. It's about generating those feelings on a daily basis and reorienting your brain, your beliefs, and your behaviours so you can feel this abundance and joy right now. You no longer have to wait to feel successful, happy or abundant. You can create those feelings daily, which will then support you as you continue to dream and grow.

Your goals now become small, manageable realities that are easy to focus on. These micro shifts allow you to not only sustain the changes you want, but you can also actually see your growth in leaps and bounds. No more story about "I'll be happy when." You can be happy today and take control of you experiences, your business and your life.

As a holistic entrepreneur, you know that your business is an extension of you. Wanting money and success (whatever that may mean to you) is amazing. When you embody those feelings and dreams daily, you will see those successes in all areas of your life, and it becomes easier to be more successful.

The Procrastination Game.

Procrastination is that strange habit we all have of putting something off for later.

Why do we procrastinate? The answer is easy, the fear of doing it outweighs the priority or reward that we will get by completing it.

As a holistic entrepreneur, you will procrastinate. It's a normal human behaviour. There are things that we have to do that can be hard or scary or uncomfortable.

Do you always file your taxes on time? Ever put off a hard conversation? The satisfaction of doing these actions might be great. Or we might not get the response we want. You might get a big tax bill, or someone will disagree with you and tell you so. Either way, our fear, our what ifs, our "it's not worth my time or energy", all lead us into putting things off.

Procrastination could be a really big deal, or it could be seen as sort of harmless. I think procrastination takes up huge amounts of mental, physical and emotional energy. This is a gigantic expenditure that wastes our resources, brain power and emotions. And if you really want to dive in deeper, procrastination is also a 3rd chakra issue. (I've got a whole chapter on chakras coming up later.)

Hot tip: *Think back to a time that you procrastinated about something. Think about how much time you spent worrying about it. How much did it rattle about in your brain, staying on your "to do "list? How many ways did you go through the various scenarios to get it done? How many options were played out for the possible different results or outcome you might get?*

When you start to categorize the cost of your procrastination and truly understand how it's hindering you, then you can decide if it's worth your time, energy and emotions to procrastinate. You can choose to put something off and not make it a priority. It's an important skill to decide what needs your attention and what can wait. That's your job as a business owner. However, if you are not in choice point and are spending time worrying about a task, that's wasting precious resources that you could be putting towards another, perhaps more beneficial, goal.

I want you to deal directly with your procrastination and fears. If something is worth getting done, prioritize it, make a plan or a SMART goal, and get it done. If you are afraid, address your fears. Maybe you need to go through the what ifs. Maybe you need a friend to be accountable to. Maybe you need outside resources. Maybe you need more information. It doesn't matter how you do it, step into it. Sit down and map out what the next steps are and get to it. Procrastination can kill your business. It will cost you money, clients and opportunities.

A SMART goal is a goal that is Specific, Manageable, Achievable, Relevant and Time Based. Look it up on the internet for more resources on how to create effective SMART goals

---

Have you heard about the 5 second rule? This rule states that if you think about something, you need to act to get it done in the next 5 seconds or it won't happen.

Let's take it a little further. You think about paying your taxes, but you are driving down the road. When you stop, pull out your phone and put a note in your calendar or a reminder saying, "get taxes done". That is an easy way to enact the 5 second rule.

How about laundry. Ever working or watching tv and think "oh, I should go change the laundry." If you don't get up and change it, it will slip off the priority list and won't happen. That's ok. Nothing bad will happen, unless your clothes are in the washing machine and you forget them overnight, in which case you will have smelly and mildewy clothes.

By activating the 5 second rule you can stop wasting time. You don't need to worry about it. If your taxes pop up into your head again, you get to reassure yourself "yeah, right, good thing I set aside Thursday night to get all that done." And you don't need to think about it again.

Getting a system in place to deal with all of these things will vastly improve your life. If you can't deal with it in 5 seconds, put a reminder in your calendar for when you can deal with it.

Finally, how about this. What if your procrastination is actually about priorities? Did you ever wonder if the reason you aren't doing your taxes is because they aren't your priority?

Let's take that idea a little bit further. What if doing your taxes isn't your priority and you make that ok?

I'm not here to give you financial advice or to advise you to not pay your taxes. I am here, though, to ask you to manage your energy. Think about how many times you let "oh, crap, I really need to do my taxes" run through your head? What are the feelings here? Guilt? Shame? Anxiety? Worried about penalties and interest? Fear of the unknown? Is this keeping you up at night?

When you realize all the emotional and mental energy that you are taking up with "I need to do my taxes", you can put yourself into choice point. Your choices are:

A) Taxes are important and I will set a time to get them done. I can hire someone or do it myself. I no longer need to worry about it.

OR

B) My taxes are not a priority. I am going to put it aside for now and come back to this in 6 months. (next year, never)

Either make it a priority, set up a plan and get it done: hire someone to do it for you, ask your partner or friend to help you, get the buddy system in place - I am doing this goal and you have that one, so let's be accountable to each other. It doesn't matter, just get it done. Give yourself a date and timeline. Set up a small step that will get you moving in the right direction. For example, I need to do my taxes so I will call my accountant for an appointment today. That's all you need to do to start moving. Don't punish yourself to get it done tomorrow. Simply start with one small step that will help you move towards that goal.

If it's not a priority, stop worrying about it. Say to yourself "This isn't my priority right now" and leave it. If you are getting swirly thoughts and they keep interfering, repeat "This isn't my priority right now."

Hot tip: *If you say something isn't a priority and have put it aside, but it still keeps buzzing around in your head, you might want to listen. Your core values, spidey senses or intuition are going off. Who cares why? Just take a moment to re-evaluate what you are experiencing and decide if perhaps you DO want to make it a priority.*

Pull it Together:

Great. You now have your mission, vision, values and goals in place. You have set aside time to work with your Embodiment Board. It's ok if this work is not perfect. Don't expect perfection. But do expect of yourself that, if you are serving your clients, they deserve for you to be committed and clear on what you're providing and why it's important. Go on, get it done. And then keep going.

And make sure you spend some time evaluating your procrastination issues. They will come up. Find solutions that work for you, or put the goal aside as not a priority. Give yourself permission here. I tell all my healer's that the only difference between success and failure is the willingness to keep trying. It's ok to get tripped up. It's ok to be afraid of something. But don't allow that to slow you down and prevent you from achieving what you want to achieve.

4

YOUR BIGGEST ASSET

Is your biggest asset your money? Your many degrees? All the years of training and experience you have had at your craft?

You are your biggest asset. Who you are, how you show up in the world and how your serve your clients, makes you unique and potent.

When you realize that you are doing the world a disservice by not showing up, sharing your gifts and delivering a kick ass product or service, you will quickly get yourself into shape and take care of you.

We are valuable, and so important in our communities and to the people around us. I believe that we are each right where we are meant to be, influencing each other, sharing our wisdom and pains and that it's all perfectly designed.

(Is it by design? I don't know.) What do you gain by acting insignificant?

If you own a coffee shop, the customers you serve are so grateful for that amazing cup of coffee.

Are you a florist? Someone cannot wait for their beautiful flowers. Or perhaps you are draping someone's casket with flowers and this can bring some relief and healing memories to the family and friends who are grieving.

Perhaps you are an artist. What joy and pleasure do people experience when they engage with your art? Music, painting, poetry, or pottery. It doesn't matter. Some feeling, and memory and joy is brought to the person who has purchased your craft. That's marvelous.

Hot tip: *How do you downplay your offerings? How do you make your business "less important"? What is the sabotage story you tell yourself?*

When you realize that you are valuable and needed in your sphere of influence, how might that change how you show up to your business? How might that change how you show up to yourself?

Ground yourself into serving the people around you. See the value you bring. Celebrate the joy you share with your offerings.

Hot tip: *Write down a list of all the little ways you bring joy and value to your community. This can be hiring staff, bookkeepers or other contractors, delivering up a great cup of coffee, sponsoring the local sports team, or donating to a charity. Maybe you have a funny sign outside your shop that makes people laugh. Perhaps you provide a safe workplace. Maybe you pride yourself in having well paid staff with incredible benefits. You need a list of at least 20 ways that you bring value to your community. 50 would be better. Keep adding to you list as you see the benefits and value you bring.*

Understanding your sabotage language and beliefs, and also cataloguing all the ways you bring joy and value to your community, is a vital aspect of your business. Successful businesses will constantly re-evaluate how they give value to their clients, their community and themselves. This is your win/win or no-go lens. Don't be afraid to be honest and fearless with this evaluation; it will make you and your business stronger and more potent.

Self-Care.

If you centre yourself as an asset, you now have to ask, how am I taking care of that asset? Self-care is glossed over; we all mindlessly skim over the articles talking about it. People keep talking about self-care like it's a bubble bath and a glass of wine.

Self-care is really about knowing yourself and what you love and doing those things, in every moment of every day. What lights you up? It's having boundaries. It's working out how you feel good. It's having sex dates. It's eating your favourite foods. It's getting the tasks done on your to-do list because you know it's worth it. It's taking out the garbage because you take care of your home and deserve the fresh smelling bag in the bin.

Until you are willing to centre yourself like the Monet you are, you will never experience the happiness and success you want to realize.

You need:

- A beautiful location to reside in (a safe home);
- A clean environment with regular maintenance;
- Other beautiful and priceless items around you (and I don't mean expensive);
- Time to be public and time to be private;
- Money that supports you to create this life;
- Security;
- Proper lighting;

- Time for deep restoration;
- Rituals and schedules that support you;
- Love and adoration.

If you take that list out of context, you could be talking about a priceless art piece in a museum or a human being. Our needs are not so different.

Ensure you have a few people who deeply love and care about you. Make time for alone time. Make time for deep rest and reflection. You need enough food, enough to pay for your home and a little more. You need a clean space. You need a beautiful home. Nothing here has to be fancy. Nothing here has to be expensive. Take a moment and evaluate what you have surrounded yourself with.

Hot Tip: *Use the list above and write down all the ways you are currently supporting yourself. List your best friends. Your pets. Write down all the ways that you have curated a life that supports you. Then notice where there might be gaps and get creative on how you can fix those gaps.*

The quickest path to business failure is owner burnout. (We are not including pandemics or floods or other disasters beyond our control). Unless and until you prioritize radical self-care, rest, relaxation and joy in your life, your business is at risk of underperforming and letting down your staff, your clients, and yourself.

Wounded Healer Archetype.

I love working in the container of archetype medicine. It helps us understand the layers and depth of the many ways we show up in the world. It's not perfect, but it helps us understand who we are and why we behave the way we do.

Archetype: In Jungian psychology, an inherited pattern of thought or symbolic imagery derived from past collective experience and present in the individual unconscious.[1]

The wounded healer archetype shows up, generally, as someone offering healing, compassion and knowing, in a space that they too, are deeply seeking and needing healing, compassion and knowing.

Many healers are drawn to their type of work due to wounding. It can be wounding from this lifetime. It might be ancestral wounds. It could be karmic wounding relating to the land you live on.

The wounded healer archetype can be extremely supportive or devastatingly harmful. It sets us up with the ability to meet our clients in a way that, perhaps, they have never experienced before. However, it also may create a dynamic where the wounded healer is unconsciously seeking to meet their own needs through the healing relationship with their client. At its worst, the wounded healer archetype shows up as the Savior or Martyr archetype. This person believes, egoically, that they can heal you - whether that is through their exalted status as a Savior with their spirituality all figured out, or in the deep sacrificial offerings of the Martyr, such as having poor boundaries and overextending themselves with the belief in the "higher good". The wounded healer can create an environment for more wounding. This dangerous dyadic relationship ensures that the client is reliant on an outsider, and the healer is only stepping in for their own personal rewards.

How do you know if you have a wounded healer archetype?

Reflect on the following statements:

- I feel called to do this work;
- I have direct, lived experience with these issues;
- I know what if feels like to have this pain;
- I have been fascinated with (insert topic here) my whole life;
- I love learning about this topic and never seem to tire of it.

Many healers have a wounded healer archetype running. It's why you were called to this deep soul medicine work.

A fundamental tenant in my Wild Medicine Healer's Training is the recognition that no one can heal you. The body has an incredible ability to create perfect homeostasis. Physically, yes, we can have challenges. Emotional and mental impacts cannot be minimized. Science is proving the profound impact that the mind / body connection has on our health. Epigenetics and other ancestral wounds, and the impacts they can have on us, are also being uncovered by science. As healers, we have a relationship with these knowings and strive to treat our clients as complex and whole humans.

When you hold your client as the expert in their own healing, honour their path as perfection and divine, and trust their journey, you allow your clients to actualize their lives in a way that is truly loving and filled with harmlessness and compassion. Your job as a healer is to hold that space and knowing for them, and to offer the tools that you have to support them on their journey. You could be a medical doctor prescribing a medication or an energy healer offering supportive insights. Both offer potent and relevant healing. That is your job as a healer.

Until you can hold yourself in a space of love, filled with harmlessness and compassion, you are actualizing the wounded healer archetype. You must have the knowing, wisdom and self-awareness to recognize your own unmet needs, and seek to do your own healing work.

Until you can see yourself as perfect and whole and a work in progress, you are most likely projecting the wounded healer archetype.

This does not need to be bad, or doom and gloom. Breathe this knowing in and see how it lands for you. Standing with your clients, in some of the most vulnerable and painful experiences of their lives, deserves our deepest respect and honouring, for ourselves and our clients.

As a healer, there are a number of important aspects we consider before standing with another and offering up this healing space.

Hot Tip: *Take a moment to evaluate your relationship with yourself in the healing realm. Ask yourself:*

1. *What is my relationship to my pain?*
2. *How do I tend to my own inner garden with love and nourishment?*
3. *Where are the shadow spaces that I am not yet ready to go?*
4. *What medicine teachings have I learned from my experience?*
5. *What lessons do I believe to be true?*

Take some time to answer these questions in your journal. Working from the unconscious, in the role as a healer, means that many of us may be seeking the healing we so desperately want and deserve in the outward actualization of our work with our clients.

Respect your relationship with your wounded healer archetype. The more you recognize it and bring it into the space, the more you can work with it honestly and with integrity.

You know you will be triggered. You know that others will be triggered by you. Deep compassion for yourself, and honouring your truths and experience, will help you to know this healer space.

Does this mean that if you identify with the wounded healer archetype, you shouldn't offer healing? Absolutely not. I truly believe we will never be healed. Life is a journey, not a destination. However, when the wounded healer is living in the subconscious, it can be making decisions for us and informing our landscape. This is another opportunity for you to be fearless in your own journey and recognize what is working for you and what might no longer be a supportive behaviour or belief.

Even if you do not offer "healing" work in your business, you know how a joyful interaction with a client can change your day. A genuine smile or an honest apology can leave two people feeling uplifted. A meeting of the minds to find a solution to a problem can be a rewarding and inspiring event. Each of these interactions offers opportunities to lift someone up, make each of us feel seen and heard and valued. This is the space of your business. Understanding the unconscious motivations and unmet needs we may have offers us greater insight and a pathway to deeper healing and more happiness.

Expert Status.

When we start to step into the space of our genius, we have to start working with the things that we are an expert at. Now, I know you are thinking you're probably not the expert at anything. Well, here is a definition of an expert:

Definition of EXPERT: *you are in a room with an average/normal/regular bunch of people. What topics do you most likely know the most about? ? (Credit to Lisa Johnson for this definition)*

You are most likely undervaluing all of your skills and experiences. Start viewing yourself in this lens and see what shows up. It's ok if this takes a little practice.

When you realize you are the expert, you also start to see where others are experts. Now that's the zone of magic.

Here's my list of expertise:

- Women's holistic health;
- Pregnancy;
- Childbirth;
- Breastfeeding;
- Women's sexual health;
- Couple issues;
- Vegan/vegetarian lifestyle;
- Homeschooling/unschooling;
- Organic foods;
- Hospital politics especially around women's health and female practitioners;
- Patriarchy;

- Pagan Rituals;
- Herbalism;
- Aromatherapy;
- Entrepreneurship;
- Blended families;
- Travel;
- Investments;
- Purchasing secondary properties in Canada;
- Divorce;
- Energy Healing;
- Tarot/Oracle Cards;
- Midwifery exams and clinical instructor;
- Intuition;
- Neuroplasticity of the brain;
- Financial Success;
- Dance instruction;
- Apprenticeship and mentorship;
- How to have a happy and successful marriage;

I wrote that list in less than 5 minutes. And guess what? There is a whole lot more. This is the exact kind of list you need to have for yourself.

Hot Tip: *take 5 minutes and write down what you are an expert in. Don't be shy. Put a timer on your phone and let yourself be creative. Don't worry if you're right. Just get down into what you know about.*

How do you feel? Proud? Surprised? Ashamed that you don't have more? Stuck? Baffled?

It's ok. What's most important is that you start to recognize all the good stuff you have learned. It could be from experience. It could be from formal education. It could be a blend of all those things. The more you realize the many ways you can support your clients and recognize that you do, in fact, have a lot to share, the more quickly you will get yourself out that place of fear and playing small.

You probably won't share all of those expert topics with your client. But you now have this incredible honouring of the skills you do have. You can weave them into your business. How can your knowledge and experience of this one thing actually support you and help you find a solution to this other problem? What life lesson have you learned on an interpersonal level, and how could that help you in your business today?

When you start to leverage all the skills and passions you have and roll them into a sphere of awesome, you become more focused on sharing these gifts and offering your solutions. This is the first step in getting out of your own way and helps you stop thinking you're inferior. It's also an incredibly holistic and organic approach to your life. You don't need to compartmentalize your gifts and knowledge. Each aspect of your life can inform the other. You get to be more you, every single day.

5

WISDOM OF THE CHAKRAS

Now that you have started to see how you are your biggest asset, you can start to evaluate all the ways that you get in your own way. Call it imposter syndrome, mindset issues, beliefs or the wounded inner child. I don't care what you call it. We are all human and are the sum total of our lived experiences, wisdom, culture and environment. Each of us is going to have blocks along the way.

What do you want to do with those blocks? Continue sabotage? Languish along in your life? Or are you ready to really claim the life you deserve?

Ok, here comes the woo. It can help us understand what's going on around us. You don't need to agree with or believe in chakras. Rather, you can work with these teachings as an analogy for what might be going on and how you might want to address it.

Color	Physical	Emotional	Mental	Spiritual	Chakra	Keyword	Symbol	Gift
Red	Energizing	Sensory awareness	Deter mination	I exist.	Root	Support	Square	Love and willpower
Orange	Anti spasmodic	Social awareness	Courage	I feel.	Sacral	Joyfulness	Circle	Creativity & Enthusiasm
Yellow	Digestant	Intellectual awareness	Confidence	I think.	Solar Plexus	Empowerment	Tri angle	Intellectual Power
Green	Dis infectant	Security awareness	Harmony	I love.	Heart	Accept ance	Nicene Cross	Self control and balance
Blue	Anti septic	Conceptual awareness	Peace	I will.	Throat	Verity	Cres cent	Faith and Inspiration
Indigo	Astrin gent	Intuitive awareness	Intro spection	I expand.	Third Eye	Perception	Star of David	Integrated Under standing
Violet	Diuretic	Spiritual awareness	Trans formation	I am.	Crown	Oneness	Lotus	Trans mutation of Desires

---

Disclaimer: Nothing in this section should be taken as medical advice and is not meant to replace expect medical diagnosis, care and treatment. Please seek the care and wisdom of your Health Care Provider before making any decisions about your health.

What are chakras? Chakras are centre of consciousness that have energy, memories, emotions and store karma. Many people are familiar with seven chakras. Some people say there are more.

Chakra is an ancient Sanskrit word that means "wheel". They are spiritual centres of power. When you understand the teachings of each chakra and how to work with them, you will quickly see where blocks, soul wounds or ancestral healing might be required and can start to work with those teachings.

Whatever your personal knowledge or relationship is to chakras, bring that into the space. Your deep skepticism is also welcome. We aren't drinking the Kool-Aid here. This is simply an opportunity to know and understand yourself better so that you can have a thriving business and an amazing life. Even if you take this section as completely theoretical, utilize these teachings as metaphor. You will be able to improve your life if you put some of these teachings into practice. The suggestions to bring balance and health back into alignment are practical, easy to do and shared here after many years of experience, both personally and supporting my clients.

The seven chakras we will work with are the Root, Sacral, Solar Plexus, Heart, Throat, Third Eye and Crown Chakra.

Each chakra relates to a colour from the rainbow. You can download the chart on page 50 here >>

https://wildmedicinewoman.ca/book-resources/.

HOT TIP: *As you read the following descriptions, write down the physical and emotional symptoms you recognize in yourself. Even better if you can link these symptoms to a time in your life, set of experiences, or another event that was going on for you.*

NOTE: Also, it should be noted here that our overemphasis and extreme focus on ableism is very harmful. If you have some of these physical or mental issues, this is not in any way an indication that you are somehow less. Further, it does not indicate that you "are not doing your work". This is a common misconception within the spiritual and energetic healing community. Our bodies are amazing and sacred. Assuming a "healthy" body means "healed" is an error.

ROOT (1st) Chakra:

The purpose of the root chakra is to give our soul physical form in this lifetime. This is where we plug into ancestral memory and trauma, and also is an important space of community and connection. As humans we deeply need human connection to survive, and the root chakra helps us to find and connect to our community.

The Root Chakra is located at the base of the spine. It includes the feet, legs, hips and includes the sacrum. On the front of the body, it starts just below the perineum, and it usually does include the lower part of the glutes and the anus.

Root Chakra disruptions can show up as:

- Diseases that run in the family;
- Weakening of the body as we approach death (this is a normal process);

- Long standing disease states;
- Autoimmune disorders;
- Deep exhaustion/burnout;
- Aches and pain not related to injury;
- Feelings of longing for community and connection;
- Feeling like an outsider;
- You get the flu or a cold regularly;
- Problems with the anus;
- Hemorrhoids;
- Deep feelings of shame;
- Congenital birth issues.

When the root chakra is balanced, nourished and the energy is running smoothly, you will find vitality, a body that runs well (with a few hiccups here and there), and vibrant and healthy community.

How to nourish your root chakra?

- Eat well;
- Sleep enough;
- Take naps;
- Exercise;
- Find 1 person who gets you;
- If you have autoimmune disorders, you may want to work on the underlying energetics of the disease you have, in conjunction with working with your physician and other healthcare professionals;
- If you want to heal the "family diseases" you will also need to work with the energetics of the disease

that is in the family (for example, heart disease means lack of love, joy or that forgiveness is needed in the family lineage. I will talk more about that under the chapter about heart chakra);

- Take the vitamins, medications or other supplements you might need;
- Rest;
- Play;
- Honour the limits of your body;

If you or someone you know was born with a physical issue at birth, it may be related to 3 issues. It could be:

- a soul issue from a previous lifetime that can now be worked with and healed in this lifetime;
- an ancestral/epigenetic pattern that would like to be worked with and healed in this lifetime;
- Finally, it could be a little bit of both.

Trust your intuition on this one. And don't worry if you don't have an answer yet. Let it reveal itself at the right time.

Sacral (2nd) Chakra:

The purpose of the sacral chakra is to provide us with creativity, community and the power of service. This is where we start to realize what our gifts are. What are our gifts to ourselves? What is our gift to humanity and the world?

The sacral chakra is also home to our sexual reproductive organs, our sexuality and is home of our five senses. It's our pleasure centre.

The location of the second chakra is from the perineum to the lower back. It includes all the sexual organs and lower organs of the abdomen.

Sacral Chakra disruptions can look like:

- Harmful sexual practices;

- Little or no sex drive;
- Infertility;
- Not knowing what we are passionate about;
- Lack of creativity;
- Depression;
- Isolation from others;
- Not enjoying the little things: the smell of a flower, a good glass of wine;
- Impairment or loss of one of the five senses;
- No joy in life;
- Lack of abundance;
- Money issues;
- Feelings of being a victim;
- Low back pain;
- Hip pain;
- Constipation or diarrhea;
- Disruptions of your moon time/menstrual cycle;
- Bladder issues, urinary tract infections;
- Kidney stones;
- Addictions;
- Extreme fear.

When the Sacral chakra is balanced and vibrant and awakened, you will find your sexuality is healthy and abundant, your creativity is flowing, you know what you are passionate about and you appreciate your five senses.

How to Nourish your Second Chakra:

- Treat your sexuality as sacred;

- Take good care of your body in that area;
- If you bleed, honour your cycles;
- Use and explore each of your five senses every day;
- Engage in creative play every day: Paint; Dance; Sing; Do cool make up; Wear something fun and unusual (even just your underwear if you don't want others to know);
- Explore sexual pleasure and know what you enjoy;
- Keep a gratitude journal and write down five things you are grateful for every day;
- Share you gifts with the world. Don't worry if it's not your career; just think of how you can share something you are passionate about. It could be as simple as a meaningful Facebook post;
- Figure out what you are afraid of and put in actionable steps to change that;
- Enjoy your pleasure with moderation. This includes alcohol, sex, food, exercise, work or any other pleasure you have;
- Give money away to strangers;
- Donate to charity.

Depression lives in the 2nd chakra. It manifests not only as a complete lack of joy, but the inability to actually use the five senses to experience pleasure. This state of depression is a complete collapse, energetically, of the chakra. This is why people who are depressed can't "just pull themselves out of it." If you are experiencing this type of depression or know someone who is, please be sure to get expert help.

The 3rd Chakra:

The 3rd chakra is our power centre. This is our space of confidence and courage. The third chakra is where we process and digest our world.

The 3rd chakra is also where we start to bring those gifts from the 2nd chakra and share them with the world. Our gifts are held and nourished and dreamed of in the 2nd. The 3rd chakra is the action centre. This is an accomplishment-oriented chakra that helps us with our willpower.

The Solar Plexus Chakra is located from the belly button to the xyphoid process (where your ribcage meets)

Solar Plexus Chakra disruptions can look like:

- Digestive upsets;
- Indigestion;
- Diarrhea;
- Long standing digestive problems;

- Inability to absorb nutrients;
- Ulcers;
- Gallstones;
- Diabetes (no sweetness in life);
- Nausea and vomiting;
- Anger issues;
- Either/or thinking;
- Things are either right or wrong;
- Can't get anything going;
- Procrastination;
- Not doing the hard things;
- Avoiding having difficult conversations;
- Hiding;
- Superiority complex;
- Anxiety;
- Lack of self-worth;
- Feelings of wanting revenge;
- Constant feelings that people undervalue you;
- Using intellect only;
- The need to control;
- Out of touch with emotions; OR
- Controlled by our emotions.

When the solar plexus chakra is balanced, vibrant and awakened, you will find that you have sustained ability to work and get things done. You are courageous enough to face your fears and do hard things. You will find that you can take in other people's ideas and feedback, even if you don't' agree. You don't feel threatened or need to be right if people don't agree with you because you know you're ok.

How to nourish your 3rd chakra:

- Eat foods that are good for you;
- Eat foods that feel good in your body too;
- Don't take things personally;
- Do things to increase your confidence;
- Dress well and look nice (for yourself);
- Listen to other opinions without feeling threatened;
- Agree to disagree;
- Drink enough water;
- Take time to have regular poos;
- Say no to things you don't want;
- Say yes to things you do want;
- Have good boundaries;
- Take the time to know what your emotions are;
- Listen to your gut;
- See and honour the value in yourself and others;
- Do something that scares you once in a while;
- List things you are proud of and write them down before you go to bed (2-3 things);
- Value yourself every day. What makes you special? Write it down;
- Try not to seek outside approval (yes, we all need it, but nourish and generate that self-esteem from the inside too).

Anxiety is at home in the 3rd chakra. This comes from an energetic collapse in this chakra. It manifests as needing to always please other people as a safety technique and coping strategy. People who suffer with anxiety actually don't know what they like, what foods they should eat and are mostly disconnected from their wants and needs. This has arisen from a complete need (generally out of survival needs) to orient themselves to others around them. In other words, if you are suffering from anxiety, you know it is not safe to be you and it's not safe for you to have any needs. You must anticipate and meet the needs of others. The deep anxiety felt is born out of a safety mechanism to anticipate every possible scenario and have a plan to deal with each possible outcome.

Anxiety is a normal emotion for many of us when we are learning something new or are out of our comfort zone. However, you can see how completely debilitating it can be and how it disrupts the ability of a person to do something positive and supportive for themselves.

If you or someone you know suffers with anxiety, please be sure to get help from your Healthcare Provider.

The 4th or Heart Chakra:

The 4th chakra is the home of love. It also houses our ability to experience and express joy. Forgiveness of self and forgiveness of others are also energetic teachings of this chakra. Grief also resides in the 4th chakra.

It is located from the xyphoid process to the collar bones.

Heart Chakra disruptions can look like:

- Heart disease;
- Cardiac issues;
- Low or high blood pressure;
- Blood disorders;
- Anemia;
- Deep grief that you cannot seem to work through;
- Anger;
- Deep hurt;
- Lung issues;

- Breathing troubles;
- Asthma;
- Inability to love others;
- Inability to love self;
- Self-hatred;
- Rage;
- Mother Wounding story;
- Always seeking pleasure outside of self (may contribute to addictions);
- Inability to self soothe;
- Unable to connect with others;
- Unable to relate to others;
- Always seeming to have very extreme relationships, from deep love to deep hatred;
- Always finding drama in your relationships;
- Not knowing what joy is;
- Seeking happiness in external circumstances;
- Not having healthy and satisfying relationships;
- Hanging onto past hurts;
- Inability to find forgiveness;
- Perfectionism in self;
- Unable to find acceptance with self
- Unable to accept others
- Hoarding.

When the heart chakra is healthy, balanced and awakened, you will have balanced and nourishing relationships. You will experience deep grief and find ways to move with it and carry it. You will have things that bring you great joy. You will feel emotionally balanced and stable. You will know how to work through the emotional ups and downs that come your way. You will love deeply. You will have healthy attachments to people you love. You will have deep compassion for yourself and others. You respect that people make mistakes (yourself included!).

How to nourish the Heart Chakra:

- Learn about healthy relationships;
- Read;
- Sing;
- Move your body for pleasure;
- Laugh;
- Really try to see another's point of view;
- Be compassionate;
- Cry;
- Grieve;
- Create rituals to honour your griefs and losses;
- Call your mother or father or grandparents;
- Write letters;
- Do a random act of kindness;
- Give yourself and others the benefit of the doubt;
- Smile;
- Forgive yourself;
- Forgive others;
- Accept yourself
- Listen to the intuition of your heart;
- Spend time with friends;
- Tell people you love them;
- Do good deeds for no reason;

- Have compassion for yourself;
- Have compassion for others.

When deep grief gets lodged in the heart chakra, it can have a profound effect on the person's ability to experience joy and pleasure. The act of radical forgiveness is not about forgiving the trespass. It is about not holding that grief and pain and anger in our heart.

Joy is very different than happiness. Joy moves freely throughout the energetic body, which is why movement and laughter are so important to the heart chakra.

Hot Tip: *Write down what joy means to you and how it is different than happiness*

Throat or 5th Chakra:

The throat chakra is the space of truth and integrity. This is the area of the body that allows our truth and new truths to be revealed. It's is a potent teaching space and sometimes manifests as surprised knowing and insights. Ever have a time when you opened your mouth and were completely surprised by what came out? That's the inspiration of the 5th chakra.

The 5th chakra acts as a gateway between our higher selves, the multiverse and our physical reality on this planet. When it is in flow, you will experience deep communication on a soul level, new reveals and information that was not yet known and creative solutions that await your implementation.

The 5th chakra is located from the collar bones to the bridge of the nose and includes the neck and shoulders.

5th Chakra disruptions look like:

- Thyroid disorders;
- Throat problems;
- Difficulty swallowing;
- Heartburn;
- Mouth problems;
- Tongue problems;
- Cavities/ Root Canals;
- Facial numbness;
- Excessive blushing;
- Feeling of lumps in your throat;
- Unable to speak your truth;
- Lying;
- Gossip;
- Stretching the truth;
- Being all in your head;
- Not trusting your intuition;
- Needing facts or science to always make your decisions;
- Unable to follow your heart;
- Doing things out of your integrity;
- Shoulder problems;
- Neck problems (a sore neck usually means you aren't looking at other points of view);
- Jaw pain;
- Ear troubles (you don't want to hear what's being said);
- Hearing loss;
- Tinnitus;

- Vertigo;
- Feeling overly burdened from family, friends or life.

When the 5th chakra is balanced, vibrant and awakened, you will find it easy to express yourself. You will trust your intuition and your inner knowing. You won't seek approval from others. You will experience a beautiful melding of science, intellect and trust. Inspired thoughts and words will flow from your mouth. Suddenly you will "know what to say" without thinking about it. Integrity will be important for you, in yourself and as a quality and trait you seek and admire in others. Truth will be a guiding principle and yet you will not feel the need to harm others with your words.

How to Nourish the 5th chakra:

- Speak honestly;
- Say the hard things;
- Sing;
- Talk to yourself;
- Write poetry;
- Read daily;
- Affirm when you see truth in other situations;
- Call in* racism, sexism, ableism, white supremacy;
- Follow your heart even in times when you mind says no;
- Trust your intuition (even when you think you shouldn't);
- Continue to feed your need to learn;

- Create a connection with Spirit/God, the Multiverse or your higher self;
- Seek out alternate viewpoints and opinions;
- Write letters that you would never send;
- Spend some time doing breathwork;
- Floss your teeth;
- Take care of your teeth;
- Open your mouth and allow the words to flow;
- Don't over think;
- Allow wisdom and lived experience to blend with intuition and heart leading choices;
- Stretch your neck.

**Calling in is the term I use instead of the "call out". I love the idea of bringing people together with new ideas and sharing how something they might be saying or doing is harmful.*

The biggest challenge for people struggling with 5th chakra issues is the inability to speak their truth for fear of judgment or relying solely on their intellect. When you work with the chakra and feel its flow and ease, you will experience this balanced state and ease.

Third Eye or 6th Chakra:

The 6th chakra is all about intuition. This is that sweet spot where we can channel higher truths and knowings. These truths and knowings may be inspired by God/Spirit/The Multiverse or your higher self. They may be soul knowings. They could be the Holy Spirit. This space is where we can know the unknowable. Energetically, our third eye helps us to connect us to the Oneness and the Multiverse. If none of those resonate with you, maybe it is helpful to frame this in the context of connection with your higher self.

When something comes out of your mouth (5th chakra) and you surprise even yourself, this is a radical act of the 6th chakra flowing and moving out in the world. That's the medicine and teaching of the 6th chakra.

The 6th chakra is located from the bridge of the nose to the top of the head, just above the hairline.

6th Chakra Disruptions look like:

- Never trusting yourself;
- Hearing intuition and thinking you're crazy;
- Saying you don't have intuition;
- Being lost in the emotions and burdens of others;
- Feelings of being an "empath" and unable to balance yourself;
- Overwhelmed by fear, sadness or grief that doesn't feel like yours;
- Headaches;
- Vertigo (Dizziness);
- Eye pain;
- Seeing stars;
- Migraines;
- Recurrent headaches;
- Disruptions of vision;
- Deep grief for ecological disasters and climate change.

When the 6th Chakra is balanced, vibrant and awakened, it feels like it is easy to trust your intuition. You won't judge yourself if your intuition is "wrong". You won't need your intuition to be "right". You will easily allow the flow between getting your intuitive thoughts out to the world through your 5th chakra. You will feel confident by applying your own wisdom and experience though your intuitive experiences.

How to Nourish the 6th Chakra:

- Write down your intuitive hits and just witness when you are "right";
- Detach from your need to be "right";
- Trust the diving timing of yourself and the multiverse;
- See the completeness of the world;
- Trust the timing of other people;
- Write down your dreams (this is part of your intuitive language);
- Spend just 5 minutes in meditation;
- Go outside everyday;
- Spend some significant time in nature (walks, camping, beach days);
- Start to make small decisions based on your intuition or gut feelings (start REALLY small if you are anxious, do you want vanilla ice cream or chocolate?);
- Let yourself be wrong;
- Trust that what you need to know will be shown to you;
- Pray to your Ancestors.

Working with Your Intuition: Many holistic entrepreneurs are extremely intuitive and empathic. We easily pick up on the subtle energies and feelings of others around us. Sometimes, people will be so tuned in to others that they are often drained, overwhelmed, sad or upset and don't know why. This is often a sign that you don't actually know how to ground, cleanse and breathe properly.

Everyone is intuitive. We have all walked into a room and realized there was a huge fight or something big just happened. We have had those gut feelings to turn left or take a different route on our drive home, only to realize there was a big accident. Ever "guessed" someone was pregnant or dreamed it before they told you?

Intuition is just a sixth sense. We all have it. We can develop it. But if you don't know how to work with it, you may find yourself overwhelmed.

Hot Tip: *If you think that you could use more techniques to help you not be so vulnerable to other people's energy, check out my video teaching here.*

https://wildmedicinewoman.ca/book-resources/

Many people believe that if they don't stay tuned in to their intuition, they will miss important information or signals that they need to know. Don't worry. I guarantee that you intuition will always kick in to keep you safe. If you need to know something, it will find a way to communicate with you. However, until you illuminate on what's your intuitive knowing and what is other people's energy, fears and emotions, you will be in an energetic overwhelm. This energetic glut will leave you flooded with energetic information that will debilitate you.

Learning to tune into your 6th chakra, understanding your intuitive language and acting on this information is a lifelong process. You don't need to make all your decisions from this space; however, this is how you move into your Zone of Genius. When you start to take leaps that don't seem to make sense or you cannot rationalize, yet feel so driven to do so, you've stepped off the cliff and into that space of radical and impressive dreaming. What might show up here will probably surprise you.

The 7th or Crown Chakra:

The 7th Chakra exists simply to connect us to the Multiverse.

God. Spirit. Oneness. Jesus. Buddha. Allah. Humanist values. Our higher selves. Our ancestors.

Whatever your spiritual reality is, this chakra connects you profoundly and divinely to this realm. This is the space of spirit guides, teachers, universal love, deep connection and Divine knowing.

The 7th chakra is located from just above the forehead to about 6-8 inches above your head.

Signs of 7th Chakra Disruption:

- Feeling alone (and scared about it);
- Obsession with death and dying;
- Very fearful of death;

- Obsessive reading about power, energy, and wanting to control it;
- Negative relationship to energy and energy healing;
- Abuse of power and trying to control the world and others around us;
- Hopelessness;
- Thinking humans are superior;
- Little respect for nature, animals and our world;
- Thinking humans are the only life forms in the Multiverse;
- Spiritual Angst;
- Dark night of the soul that you cannot seem to shift out of;
- Flipping from one belief system to another, always seeking "the answer";
- Thinking there is "an answer";
- Denying your spiritual life;
- Obsessive spiritual/religious practices;
- Cult-like worship of a way of being (this could be dietary, spiritual or any other path);
- Threat of punishment if you don't live your life "right";
- Need to pay for salvation or miracles or religious standing;
- Seeing human failings and trespasses as "their spiritual choice";
- Claiming that something horrible happens because of "karma";
- Thinking there is one "right" way;
- Seeing a religion or spiritual practice as superior.

When the 7th Chakra is balanced, vibrant and awakened, you will have a deep and peaceful connection of knowing, infinite support and wild ecstatic experiences of love. Each living being will be seen as vibrant, necessary and potent. Value is placed on the macro and the micro. Each droplet of water or bug is seen as a reflection of the multiverse. You will be assured of your potency and value as well as your limitlessness and insignificance. The value of each being will be felt deeply.

If you are not spiritual, you will find the deep honouring of the here and now. You have peace around the thought that death means the end.

Now, to be clear, we are all experiencing the human condition. Any thought that you will be aligned all the time is a falsehood. However, your willingness and ability to see yourself though this lens of deep compassion will always be with you when the 7th chakra is vibrant and awakened.

Note: Many people in the spiritual world use a dangerous spiritual bypass of thinking that the horrors and trauma we commit to other humans, nature and the earth are somehow "karmically aligned". This is the worst kind of harm we can perpetuate on others. We have all the resources, technology, agricultural techniques, sanitation processes and healthcare and education options that could solve the world's problems, tomorrow. The hoarding of resources and prioritizing one way of being over another is a harmful human construct. I believe this creates huge karma for humanity. Recognizing that these prioritizations are choices and taking responsibility for these choices can be an important and powerful shift in your thinking.

Ways to Nourish the 7th Chakra:

- Prayer;
- Gratitude;
- Meditation;
- Seeing all of nature as beautiful and necessary;
- Operating from the values of harmlessness and compassion;
- Trusting the flow of your life;
- Having faith that you are being guided and supported;
- Having faith that you are not alone, even when you think you are;
- Deep breathing;
- Ecstatic Dance;
- Witnessing the many ways we are interdependent as humans;
- Witnessing how we are interdependent with our natural world;
- Studying your spiritual or religious teachings deeply;
- Devoting yourself to your spiritual practices daily;
- Studying scientific journals: most scientist don't believe we are alone (Welcome Star Nation).

Hot tip: *write down all the ways you show up to your fellow humans, nature and the earth. What else can you do to help hold each living being in harmlessness and compassion?*

Healing Your Chakras:

You should now have a nice list of ways that your chakras might be out of alignment and inspiration of how to nourish them.

Getting your energies aligned takes time, practice and devotion. This is not because it is hard; it is because we live in a culture and society that is so far from what we need. Starting very slowly and committing to the practice daily will help you.

Don't "throw everything at it." Choose 1 or 2 things you can do easily and regularly. Start there, and evaluate how you feel after about a week. This will give you a real chance to see some change and growth.

You can build on your successes by adding something new or making a slight change every week. The sooner you start to tend to your energy, the sooner you will see big shifts and changes, both within yourself and in your community around you.

And if suddenly something pops up and you feel out of alignment, you can quickly refer back here to see what you can do to start nourishing yourself immediately. It could be stopping and taking some breaths. It could be eating nourishing food.

Hot tip: *Write down how it feels to know that you can do some other things to support yourself, even if you are physically sick or struggling emotionally. Empowered? Is this too weird for you? Maybe it's all a bunch of feel-good baloney to you? Excited to try it?*

The best part of knowing what's happening for you energetically is that now you can identify where you need some extra support, and leverage that support to help you in your business.

I remember when I was struggling to get good copywriting. I needed to redo my webpage, I was struggling to write my sales page and things just were not flowing. I knew this was a 5th chakra issue and yet I couldn't figure out how to shift out of it.

I had a copywriter that I was working with at the time. He was back and forth with me, evaluating and talking to me about my work. And I remember when it finally clicked. He said "Nadine, you're funny and gregarious and this just isn't coming across in your writing."

Boom. That was the mirror moment I needed to understand where and how I was blocked. I was following a formula. I had never written good copy before. I was reading how to write "copy that converts" and following step-by-step processes, but it wasn't me. I sat down and wrote my copy out that afternoon. It was easy. It just flew.

I wasn't trusting myself. I wasn't listening to my heart. I needed to trust my throat chakra and my 6th chakra (my intuition) that the words were there, that my voice was good and solid and true and let it flow.

That is the power I want you to step into in your own business. Know yourself and align with your superpowers. They will ebb and flow. The more quickly you recognize when you are out of alignment, the easier it will be to correct what's happening and get back to the business of serving your clients.

Please remember, none of these writings replace good, competent healthcare. These teachings are here to offer you a new and adjunct way to support yourself so you can realize the life, joy and wellness you deserve.

6

MONEY MAGIC

How did you feel when you read the title of this chapter? Happy? Sad? Anxious? Did you think it was stupid?

Your first reaction to money is a great clue to help you understand your relationship to money.

Hot tip: *Take 1 minute (time it on your phone) and write down all the feelings and ideas that come into your head when you think about money. Do not evaluate or judge. Just brainstorm.*

Money is simply energy. When we were living in tribal times, the exchange of goods and services was normal in our communities. It was recognized that we relied on each other. Interdependence was the name of the game. The good of the many was dependant on each person contributing with their gifts, medicine, wisdom and skills.

Now we live in a society that prides itself on independence. We don't trade goods for services, it's all about a monetary exchange.

While I am not necessarily advocating that we return to bartering, I would invite you to shift your money mindset to how it would feel if your service and product were essential to the wellbeing of the group? What happens if you also treat the goods and services you purchase as essential to the wellbeing of your community?

This small energetic shift can dramatically change how you feel about money.

When we walk out of the hair salon with a new haircut? We feel and look amazing.

When we pay for and listen to a beautiful piece of music? We might have soothing feelings of joy and pleasure.

When you buy a new toilet brush? Yes, you get to crap in a clean toilet. Thank you, toilet brush gods.

When we book a luxurious suite in a high-end hotel? Juicy goodness, luxury, pampering, self-care, and maybe you feel a little indulgent.

Not only can you celebrate your feelings of abundance and well-being, someone else also benefited from your purchase.

You may have a money mindset that says, "this item is luxury" and "this item is necessary". That's ok. The invitation here is to move to the interdependence we have on each other. When you buy that toilet brush, especially from the local hardware store, there are real humans that are appreciating your business. This energetic shift to interdependence will help you clean up your idea of rich and poor. Each of us is essential. See the value of the humans on the end of your purchases. Imagine putting money into the pockets of real people when you buy something, big or small. Breathe into that. How does it feel?

If you really want to get wild here, also try to buy local. Boutique hotels. Go to the health food store, not Costco, for your vitamins. I know you might be thinking "privilege" and it's true, some people may have extra money to spend at higher cost stores. But allow yourself to even just go to the local bakery instead of Starbucks. These simple and small acts quickly add up. Your energetic relationship to money will start to shift when you see the real relationship you have with it, and your community.

What does money mean to you? What opportunities does money offer you and your family? Money is simply one more tool for me to create the life I want. And, most importantly, I was happy when I was poor.

I remember being so poor that I had to count out every nickel and penny so I could buy my children milk. I remember scrounging in the sofa for money. Crying when that unexpected bill came, or a kid came home from school with a field trip form and a $20 price tag. I didn't have the money. But I was happy.

My husband and I were wildly in love. My kids were doing ok, in spite of a messy divorce. I had a nice rental home that I could barely afford, but I could afford it. I didn't go out for coffee for 2 years. I didn't drink alcohol unless someone brought over beer or a bottle of wine. I didn't have cable tv. I had food. I was practicing midwifery, which I loved. It was hard. Really hard. And I was extremely happy.

Hot Tip: *Evaluate now if you have an "I'll be happy when" story. Write it down. Remember, no judgement or shame here.*

Money just makes life easier. Research tells us that we need enough to pay our bills and then a little bit more for fun, play and silliness.

Get happy now. Start to make the changes you need in your life. Nurture healthier relationships, exercise more or drink more water. These are simple and easy steps that can improve yourself. Get off your phone and read a book. Call a friend. Go for a walk. Take a bath. Start doing things that are free and nourishing and loving to yourself. Take good care of you and see what shows up next. Go back to your Embodiment Board and see what feelings you want to generate more of. How can you do that today? Get creative and see how the abundance will start to flow to you.

I am convinced that one of the reasons that I didn't stay in that extreme poverty was:

#1 I had faith that I could improve my life; and

#2 I wasn't relying on a crappy constructed reality (money) to make me happy.

I see money as just one more tool that can help me live the life I want and also help me to support and serve others.

Unpack your Money Story.

There are so many ways that our money story impacts us, and we are unaware of many of them. Reviewing your money story gives you an opportunity to evaluate what's working for you, what's not and get a plan in place to change things. This is one more area that the RAS has pre-programmed for you. This programming is based on your family, culture, religion or spiritual beliefs and where you grew up.

Money is a big word. It's loaded. It conjures up all kinds of feelings of self-worth, success, power, and shame. In a consumer-based culture, we are bound to feel those negative feelings if we don't measure up to the "success" markers of our community, city, class or culture. Each of those success markers form our own, usually internalized, definitions of success. We will be vulnerable to those outer guideposts if we don't do some serious work on our relationship with money.

Hot tip: *Money is only energy. And there are LOTS of other forms of energy too. Sunshine, food, air, water, love. Write down the energies that are abundant in your life right now. Include things that are overly abundant (too much conflict at work) and may also harming you.*

I have a client who started an extremely successful business, selling second hand and vintage clothes. This client was passionate about the values of reduce, reuse and recycle. There was also firm knowledge on the harms of "fast fashion" and sweatshops that are exploiting people around the globe. My client was able to monetize their passions and their values on these principles.

In my client's community, these second-hand clothes are the bomb. There are huge fashion statements to be made with wearing a particular type of shirt with special tags. Vintage shoes are sold for hundreds of dollars. Now for me (and maybe you too) I wore this stuff in the 80's and 90's. It probably isn't that flattering on me now, as an almost 50-year-old woman. Yet my client and their community know exactly what is cool and hip. In their community, these items of clothing make them stand out and are also a statement of who they are and what their values are.

We all want to fit in and be seen as a good and worthy person. Recognizing how this need to fit in plays a role in our money mindset can help us to understand who we are and what we want.

It's time for you to get the journal out. As a holistic entrepreneur, you have to get real with your money beliefs. Until you understand what you believe and what's motivating you, you will struggle with hidden and unconscious beliefs. The RAS will be on high alert to only allow in money beliefs that fit in the current file. I want to help you make some new and robust files.

Money Beliefs:

Take a few minutes and read the following questions. Write down your answers. They can be brief, or you can spend an hour or two here. Just make sure that you answer as honestly as you can. You might get triggered. You might get angry. You might feel sad and dig up some old hurts. Make space for big feelings when doing this exercise so you can dig deep and know what's motivating your behaviour.

Growing up money beliefs:

- What was the money story growing up in your family?
- How did your family deal with money?

- What gender roles did you witness as a child relating to money, including your grandparents?
- How did your family talk about money?
- Did you worry about money or food when you were a kid?
- What are your memories of other kids in school? Who was rich? Who was poor?
- How were rich kids treated at school?
- How were poor kids treated at school?
- What religious or spiritual rules were there about money as you were growing up?
- What ways were you overlooked in school?
- What ways were you overlooked at home?
- In what ways did you have to sacrifice for others?
- Did you have an allowance?
- Did you have a job as a teenage?
- What kinds of vacations did you have growing up? Did you think they were good?
- When did you realize where your family sat on the wealth spectrum in your community?
- o When did you realize you were a "poor" family?
- o When did you realize you were a "rich" family?
- o When did you realize you were a "middle class" family?
- How did the realization of where you slotted in on the "financial success" spectrum make you feel?
- What is your favourite memory as a child in relation to money? (or gifts?)

Adult Experiences:

- Did you go to college or university?
- Did you buy your first car?
- Was your first car a gift?
- Do you forgo the finer things in life?
- How would you classify yourself now? Are you rich? Poor? Average?
- Do you think others have more than you?
- Do you save money regularly?
- Do you have loads of debt (not related to your housing)?
- Do you own a home?
- Do you have a job?
- Are you remunerated properly for your work?
- Do you struggle to make ends meet?
- What is a symbol of wealth and success in your culture and community?
- If I gave you $25,000 right now, what would you do with it?

Partner Influences with money:

If you are not currently in a partnership, consider how you would want your relationship to look like in relationship to these questions.

- How does your partner show up to money?
- Does your partner have a job?
- Do you and your partner fight about money?

- Do you and your partner argue about how much "extra" money there is to spend at the end of the month?
- Who makes most of the financial decisions in your relationship?
- Who is "better with money" in the relationship?
- Who is the "spendthrift" or "wild one" when it comes to money?
- Who values stuff more?
- Who values experiences more?
- Where did your partner grow up on the wealth spectrum?
- Do your backgrounds match when it comes to relationships with money?

Obviously, this list could go on and on. However, I hope you are starting to see the variable influences that are around you. You should be getting more clarity on what your beliefs and values are about money.

Wherever you are on the money spectrum, this is just an honouring and auditing of your current beliefs and relationship to money.

Any surprises? Anything jump out at you? Did any painful memories or experiences show up?

Michael and I have been married for 15 years and together for almost 19 years. It's the relationship that I always wanted, and I manifested it. But as we started doing more couple things, my old money patterns were showing up.

Michael really likes managing the money. He's also really good at it. He doesn't lie, cheat, or scam on his taxes. He certainly doesn't control my access to the money in our family. So, this is all really good stuff. Until I realized it wasn't. I was abdicating my relationship with money. I wasn't staying engaged. I wasn't taking responsibility. Yes, I earned money and yes, I wasn't too reckless, but I wasn't as responsible and engaged as I could be.

When I realized that my belief about money in marriage was that men manage the money and women spend it, I got to decide if I wanted to keep that belief or change it. It doesn't' mean it was bad or wrong. I just realized that if I wanted to be more in abundance, I wasn't going to create that by burying my head in the sand and letting someone else be responsible for creating it.

Money issues are often 2nd chakra issues. Also, clearly, I had some beliefs around men and women in relation to money. These beliefs probably came from where I lived growing up, the gender roles in my family, birth order, and religious upbringing, as well as race. My experiences as an adult would have solidified those experiences, whether they were good or bad. We each bring into our lives that what we know. Remember the RAS? It's hard at work here. It's comfortable and safe. We know the rules and what the expected outcomes are. This doesn't mean your beliefs are perfect and it also doesn't mean that we are destined for a crap life. And the minute you understand that your brain makes sense of the world in a way that you know and that is easier for you, it allows you to see where you are operating, and then make some focused choices to create the life you want.

If I can bring compassion to those formative narratives about money, without judgement or criticism, it neutralizes my emotions. When I am amped up, angry, and resentful I am applying powerful emotions to the experience. It's fine to have any emotions that relate to your experiences and beliefs. And if you can just see these beliefs as a natural manifestation of the sum total of your life, up to this point, it gives you greater power to start shifting immediately.

I worked with forgiveness, including forgiving myself. I took targeted actions that I did daily to shift my relationship. These included checking our finances every morning, reviewing our investments, and discussing financial projections for the next week with Michael. I also started goal setting with our money for things that were important to me. With these simple actions I was able to shift my relationship with money and abundance.

Don't make yourself bad or wrong. You can take a deep dive and uncover all your wounding and hurts if that feels important to you. And you can also take small steps right now that will help you get where you want to go. Either way you choose to show up here is perfect.

What I don't want you to do is bring in the shame card. Shame for where you grew up. Shame for your behaviour. Shame for the beliefs and values you hold today. This is the best you can do right now. Maya Angelou said, "When you know better you do better". Let that be true for you.

Hot Tip: *Go through and decide which money beliefs are helpful and you would like to keep. Put those on one side of a piece of paper. On the other side, list the beliefs and experiences that were hurtful and harmful. You may want to shift those and integrate the wisdom of those lessons.*

Finally, write down any money beliefs you are interested in bringing into your life. It could be a long list or a short one. Just make sure that your paper reflects what you have that you want to keep, what invitations to healing and release around money beliefs you want to work with and finally, what other supportive beliefs are missing from your list.

Once you have this list, go back to your Embodiment Board. How is money represented on your board? Return to your journal. What are the emotions you are cultivating with those items that represent money?

Now consider how you can start to cultivate those feelings now. Abundance. Success. Wealth. Status. Security. Take a few moments here to flesh out your Embodiment Board so you can deepen your relationship with these feelings, now that you uncovered what you really want in relation to money. Also consider, is there anything that you might want to remove from your Embodiment Board because it was being motivated by a negative money belief?

Tidying up your money mindset can be easier than you think. It takes dedication. Commit to doing one thing every day that is focused on your money mindset, and cultivate those feelings. It can be 10 seconds or 10 minutes. Length of time doesn't matter. The commitment to the feelings is what will help you embody who you are and what you want.

7

MONEY ARCHETYPES

If you have a challenging relationship to money, you are probably suffering from one of two money archetypes: the unworthy archetype, or the victim archetype. Let's dive in and see which one might be preventing you from showing up and experiencing the abundance you deserve. We all deserve abundance.

Go through the following examples and check which ones you notice in yourself. You will most likely not have all of the qualities listed, and some of them might seem extreme. Reflect on how you behaved as a teenager and young adult. You might not be doing some of these things now but had these behaviours in the past. Be as honest with yourself as you can.

You won't do all of the things identified here. You might not do very many at all. This checklist might blow your mind when you realize all the ways your money beliefs and stories are running the show. Once you recognize all the ways your life experience and stories become your ingrained beliefs, you can start to work with them and decide if you want to keep them or change them.

Be sure when doing the checklist that you are extremely gentle with yourself. No one has to know what your deepest secrets are, and the more honest you get with yourself, the quicker you will be able to actively work with these beliefs and see the results in your personal life and your business.

Unworthy archetype:

This archetype comes from stories and experiences that reinforce that you are unsuitable and undeserving of what you want.

This can show up as:

- Not getting what you wanted for Christmas;
- Not getting nice birthday presents;
- Always having ill-fitting or not nice (holes, ripped or stained) clothes;
- Being told you should be grateful for what you have;
- Always going last: last for food, drinks etc.;
- Taking really good care of your stuff because you fear you won't be able to replace it;
- Feeling like you need be sure others are ok first

before you can get what you want;

- Prioritizing other people's needs before your own;
- Agreeing to pay for or buy something that you can't afford because someone else wants it;
- Denying yourself things you want and can afford;
- Buying things to make you feel better and then regretting it;
- Not knowing what you really like;
- You defer to other's ideas;
- Shopping at stores you don't like when you could afford more expensive stores;
- Making do with what you have (even though you don't like it and could afford something else);
- Manipulation to get what you want;
- Feelings of greed;
- Arrogance;
- Feeling like it's never enough;
- You were picked last at school for sports, for plays or other events;
- You felt like your parents favoured another child over you;
- You felt like you weren't popular, pretty or in the "in" crowd, growing up;
- If you feel jealousy, it will stir up feelings of anger
- Being bullied for your clothes or being poor or living in the *wrong* neighborhood;
- You used to feel disappointed when you didn't get what you wanted, now you are resigned to it;
- You are more of a "behind the scenes" type person;

- You pretend you don't really value money or material things;
- You are a people pleaser;
- You might track your finances but somehow there is never any money for you;
- You're genuinely happy for others when you see their successes and wonder what their secret is (and you figure you probably couldn't do it anyways);
- You might procrastinate.

The unworthy archetype is an energetic collapse within the 3rd chakra. There is a defeatist energy here; things are bad and have been rough and they probably can't get better. The experience here is that your ask is too big, and it's actually harmful to the people around you. When you are carrying this energy, it will be very difficult for you to even know what you want or need. There is no point asking or dreaming about what you want because it will just leave you with disappointment.

This collapse is very harmful because it leaves you open to manipulation and always meeting the needs of others. It takes away your power energy to help you change and manifest what you want. And remember, anxiety lives here so what do you think people who have an unworthy archetype running also experience? Lots of anxiety.

If this sounds like you, congratulations. Now you know. We will get more on how to work with this and heal it so you can create the money and abundance in your life. You deserve it. (I know, you totally just rejected that statement… that's ok, stick with me.)

I worked with an entrepreneur who had purchased a successful company. They were the CEO. Their work ethic was great. Revenue was fairly good and consistent. Staff were committed and the product was excellent. The company's reputation within the industry was sound. However, it became very apparent that there was something going on that was resulting in hundreds of thousands of dollars a year in lost revenue.

Once we pinpointed the "unworthy" archetype running, we could get to work. This was a fascinating process because all the ways this unconscious belief was permeating the team suddenly became clear. As the leader, the CEO realized they had set the tone in the company's relationship to money. This dictated how hard the team worked to generate and collect money and it also set up an agreement of how the client could treat the company. In no way was this a conscious decision. These choices were based on years of beliefs, family conditioning, cultural values and personal experiences. The corporate culture was also present before my client bought the company. We are the sum of all these things and often have no idea how much they affect us and our choices on a daily basis.

There was a wafting culture of "unworthiness" flowing through the company. When the CEO realized all the ways this was affecting the team, they got to work. Little shifts were made in processes, operations, contractual agreements and other systemic processes. Team meetings were had with review of contracts, cash flow and the core values of the company were communicated to the team. This yielded huge results for my client. The company has seen a 300% increase in their revenues.

The most critical part of this journey was the work the CEO did on themselves. They had to get clear on their money blocks. They had to re-evaluate their goals and relationship to money. They had to recognize what needs they were meeting within themselves to have this archetype running in the first place. Believe me, no one is picking something negative. We choose these patterns because they work for us in some ways. Bringing awareness to these beliefs allows us to evaluate what's working and what isn't.

Most importantly, my client had to re-evaluate their "why". Until you understand your why, you will underperform. If you are trying to please people (unworthy archetype) you will avoid conflict. You might say yes to things that are really hard to deliver. You might not have great boundaries. You will "throw something in" that might not really be ok for you, but you do it to get the sale, to keep the peace, or be seen as the nice person.

When you reorient your why to win/win, you can shift out of the unworthy archetype and see how you are winning and being successful, and how that contributes to your client's success too. This will be hard for you because that people pleasing energy is running hard, but once you start to shift it, your clients will respect you more and you will be clearer on providing them with a great service or product and a superior customer experience.

The Victim archetype shows up as:

- No one sees your worth, so why bother;
- No one knows how awesome you really are;
- You feel like you are always undervalued;
- Hoping your wealthier friends/family will pay for you;
- Never offing to pick up the bill when out with friends;
- Stealing;
- Price tag changing;
- Taking on mounds of debt you have no idea how you will pay off;
- Spending to impress others;
- Spending to keep up with the Jones (you *think* you should have something);
- You act poorer than you are to get sympathy;
- You think others have way more than you do;
- You ask for loans from others and never pay them back;
- You are often late paying your bills;
- You would prefer to have your head in the sand about your finances;
- You can't figure out why you never get the raise/promotion at work;
- People never recognise your skills;

- You think you are a diamond in the rough and are just waiting to be discovered;
- Being told you want too much;
- Being told you have expensive taste;
- You think your life has been way harder than most people's;
- No one knows how much you've suffered;
- No matter how hard you try, people just don't see all the work you're doing;
- Perfectionist tendencies;
- You feel like it's never enough;
- If you feel jealous you will feel sad and resigned;
- You dream of winning the lottery;
- You have a "I'll be happy when I have X amount of money" story;
- You feel like the world owes you.

The victim archetype shows up as an energetic collapse within the 2nd chakra. Creativity is abused and exploited for your pleasure and getting stuff. The victim archetype really believes they have had it harder than other people. They have had more pain, more suffering and certainly have overcome obstacles that others could never imagine.

When you are constantly working within the victim archetype, you will notice that it's never enough. You want more and more and more. You are deeply seeking the approval and recognition of others and worse, you have attached a price tag to that approval. The person working with a victim archetype has never given themselves the compassion, adoration and congratulations they deserve.

The victim may steal, not pay taxes, and can get into some pretty sticky situations with their financial situation. This is because they truly believe they are owed, and this justifies their stealing or cheating because they are above the rules.

If this sounds like you, congratulations. This is a big archetypal energy running in your second chakra and is blocking you from receiving abundance. Now you know it and can work with it. You can start to honour yourself for all you hard work and gifts and the amazing human that you are.

I remember working with an incredibly skilled and talented healer. This person had years of experience under their belt and was also teaching others how to share healing work. The talent here cannot be overstated.

But after a few sessions with me, I knew right away there was a victim archetype running for this person. They had a story, and it was a good one.

Stories aren't excuses. And it's really important that we clarify that. The story was real. These were lived experiences. My client was also astute enough that we could get into the ancestral and epigenetic aspects of their experience. They knew these were deep running patterns and were influencing their behaviours and beliefs. And then that turned into a limiting belief too. "See all this pain and trauma here in my parents and grandparent's life? Of course, I'll never heal, make lots of money etc."

Once we were able to identify the victim archetype, it was all systems go. My client stopped telling their story. My client got active in their business offerings. My client filed their taxes. My client could suddenly see all the ways they were self-sabotaging because they were waiting for someone to see how wounded and hurt they were. They wanted to be saved, and now realized that they had the resources and network to save themselves.

Most importantly they could plug into gratitude work. If you really believe that the world owes you, how can you possibly be grateful for anything you have? What you have is never enough and this becomes a self-fulfilling prophecy.

Again, these are not conscious thoughts we are holding. Who wants to admit they are a victim? This can be a painful and deeply raw process. It's important to hold yourself with deep compassion here. Watching my client transform into this wild healer and passionate person was incredible. They started to leverage the stories of the ancestors and their own experiences as supportive teachings, rather than these limits that were holding them back. They were able to get out of the inertia that the victim archetype held them in and move into fiery and passionate action.

Hot Tip: *Now that you have a sense of which archetype might be running for you, write down how those beliefs and behaviours are showing up in your business. What policies, programs or other ways is your archetype influencing your business?*

Healing your Archetype:

Now, careful, don't fall down the rabbit hole. The examples I have used in the archetypes above are extreme. Very few of us have all of those descriptors.

Be gentle here. You are trying to uncover some deep soul wounds, ancestral and epigenetic wounding, and beliefs that no longer serve you. This is soul work and a lifelong practice. Your invitation is to work within these teachings to help them support you, rather than be a negative drawback.

You have been courageous enough to get this far. These patterns and beliefs are just that, patterns and beliefs. This isn't who you are. You can change your behaviours. No one needs to peer into your deepest and darkest secrets. Go slowly and gently and be honest with yourself. Let the truth ring out. The more honest you can get here, the more quickly you can create interruptions in these patterns and change your experience.

UNWORTHY Archetype HEALING:

Working with, and healing the unworthy archetype needs to start with micro steps to help you see your worth.

I have put the list here to help you see how you can nourish your 3rd chakra. Pick the smallest and easiest thing here and do it for a week. Every day. Small and simple wins.

How to nourish your 3rd chakra:

- Eat foods that are good for you;
- Eat foods that feel good in your body too;
- Don't take things personally (assume it's not about you);
- Do things to increase your confidence;
- Dress well and look nice (for yourself);
- Listen to other opinions without feeling threatened;
- Agree to disagree;
- Drink enough water;
- Take time to have regular poos;
- Say no to things you don't want;
- Say yes to things you do want;
- Have good boundaries;
- Take the time to know what your emotions are;
- Listen to your gut;
- See and honour the value in yourself and others;
- Do something that scares you once in a while;
- List things you are proud of and write them down before you go to bed (2-3 things);

- Value yourself every day. What makes you special? Write it down;
- Try not to seek outside approval (yes, we all need it, but nourish and generate that self-esteem from the inside too).

The truth is, this is really about building up your confidence. Your confidence can look different than other peoples'. You get to shine in your unique way. But right now, you really think that you just got what you got, and some people are luckier than others.

Confidence is a superpower. Fake it 'till you make it actually works when it comes to confidence.

Here is my confidence checklist. When you start working with this you might feel uncomfortable, tell yourself that it won't work for you or that this is all stupid. That's ok. Let those thoughts and feelings live here. We aren't trying to get rid of them. What we want to do is give you a choice. Right now, you don't think you have one. The minute you move into choice point, you create the space to choose something new and different.

Go through the checklist below. Choose 2 or 3 that you can really enjoy and start working with daily. You need to commit to yourself. Be easy here. Choose the ones that really resonate right off the bat. Implement them. Commit for the next 7-10 days and then re-evaluate.

Nadine's Confidence Checklist:

- Good morning routine;
- Gratitude journal you write in daily;
- Spiritual rituals;
- Exercise regularly;
- Good, nourishing sex;
- Enjoy your hobby;
- Volunteer or donate;
- Write weekly wins;
- Evaluate what you are an expert in*;
- Go outside;
- Grounding regularly;
- Good sleep routines and hygiene;
- Learn something new;
- Look good for yourself;
- Meditate;
- Read;
- Daily affirmations;
- Smile just for yourself;
- Do one thing just for you;
- Set goals for the day;
- Schedule fun;
- Have a good evening routine;
- Date yourself;
- Spend time with loved ones.

*Review your expert list in the previous chapter

You can always add your own. This is just a nice list to get you started. The minute you commit to your confidence building, you will see some improvement. And then will doubt yourself. Remember the RAS is always running. It's constantly pointing out all the ways you are not confident and will be quick to point out your mistakes and errors. Put some effort into shifting your RAS. It's going to take time and practice.

The multiverse helps those who help themselves. When you start moving towards these goals, you will see the future take a different shape, feel and smell. The multiverse honours effort. Put the effort in and track your wins.

For people with the unworthy archetype I am going to tell you a secret; you miss your wins. You miss how amazing you are. You are overlooking your awesomeness. Maybe you were rewarded for your humility. Maybe you felt that the weight of the world was on your shoulders and by sacrificing your needs you could actually help. You probably are really good at knowing what others need and want and most likely got rewarded for this skill.

"You're so compassionate", "You really get me", "Wow, you really know people", "You hardly every complain". Any of those sound familiar?

While these are noble pursuits, they might not make you happy.

I am not suggesting that you jump into the world and go buy an expensive sports car that you can barely afford (but if you did do that, I would be proud of you). But honestly, that does feel a little out of character. What I do want is for you to start counting all the ways you did well. Write it down. Journal it.

Hot Tip: *Every day you need to write down five things that you are proud of that you did that day. It could be that you didn't speed. It could be that you had a shower. It could be that you bought an expensive coat for yourself. Maybe you made a donation to a charity. No matter how big or how small, start documenting what you did in your day that you are proud of. On days that this feels hard, write down "I got to work, I didn't kill my kids, I made lunch for myself, I peed in the toilet." Do you see where I am going? On the bad days it's even more important to celebrate and honour the small things we do regularly.*

Do you see how you are missing your awesomeness? Are you uncomfortable? That's ok, you'll get used to being in love with yourself and not thinking you're some egoic freak who's full of themselves. Your family and community will be astounded. They knew you were a good egg and now you're bringing even more awesome to the game.

How could this help your business? What value might this add? It might not just be monetary gains. It could reap huge rewards for your staff. You could generate more income with less hours and hard work. Dream a little here; imagine how healing this part of your mindset your support your business. What's the win/win or no-go for your business?

Victim Archetype Healing:

The hardest thing for people with the victim archetype to learn is compassion. They don't have a lot of compassion for others, often because they have almost none for themselves.

You will need to start with compassion building and get over the "poor me" tendencies. Remember, victim energy lives in the 2nd chakra. You will need to get passionate about healing the wounds here.

How to Nourish your Second Chakra:

- Treat your sexuality as sacred;
- Take good care of your body in that area;
- If you bleed, honour your cycles;
- Use and explore each of your five senses every day;
- Engage in creative play every day:Paint; Dance; Sing; Do cool make up; Wear something fun and unusual (even just your underwear if you don't want others to know);
- Explore sexual pleasure and know what you enjoy;
- Keep a gratitude journal and write down five things you are grateful for every day;
- Share you gifts with the world. Don't worry if it's not your career; just think of how you can share

something you are passionate about. It could be as simple as a meaningful Facebook post;
- Figure out what you are afraid of and put in actionable steps to change that;
- Enjoy your pleasure with moderation. This includes alcohol, sex, food, exercise, work or any other pleasure you have;
- Give money away to strangers;
- Donate to charity.

You learned early on that you needed to take what was yours because it was never going to be given to you. You need to start so small and gently and give yourself the compassion, spaciousness and love you deserve. Until you realize that you can generate these feelings for yourself, you will always feel like you never get enough love, enough recognition or enough happiness in your life.

Nadine's Compassion Checklist:

- Give yourself compliments in the mirror every morning;
- Start soothing yourself with "good enough" statements ;
- Eat what you want to eat;
- Drink what you want to drink;
- Accept compliments as genuine (turn off any "it's about time" or "what do they want from me" stories);

- Write down when someone give you that compliment;
- Say thank you;
- See when you belonged (it's more often than you think);
- Listen when others are telling their pain stories without sharing yours (you will be surprised how grateful people will be for the listening ear);
- See something beautiful every day and write it down;
- Smell something delicious and write it down;
- Drink something precious (especially water) and write down how it made you feel;
- Add affirmations to your water bottle (write them on paper and tape them to the outside) and drink them throughout the day;
- Listen to your favourite song once a day;
- Write down your accomplishments every day;
- Include something that didn't quite meet your expectations or standards but was still ok;
- Be your natural self;
- Give yourself permission to say no;
- Give yourself permission to say yes;
- Do something just for you and don't tell anyone;
- Set a goal for something you dearly want and save or make a plan to get it;
- Go to bed when you are tired;
- Listen to the needs of your body.

One you start riding the compassion train, you will never get off. You have been so hard on yourself. How does it feel to take a breath, have some space and just be good enough, exactly as you are?

If you believe "life is hard", it will be. This is your chance to bring ease and grace into your life. This doesn't mean you won't struggle. What it does mean is that you will create a new way of showing up in your life. You will recognize when you need to give yourself a break. And suddenly you won't be so hard on the people around you. They can breathe too. You are creating a whole new way of being in the world, not just for yourself, but for your community.

What does it feel like to imagine that you are just fine, right here, right now? How does it feel to know that your pain and suffering is real and no one else has to honour that? How does it feel to know that when you start to have deep compassion for yourself, you will be able to transform your grief and hurts into compassionate teaching and inspired mentorship for others?

Hot tip: *Write down all the ways you were compassionate to yourself every night. You need at least five things. Didn't beat yourself up for being late? Good one. How about apologized for missing that email? Yeah, that's cool too. What about taking the time to download your favourite album to your phone? Bliss.*

Stop being so hard on yourself. Allow yourself the grace and compassion that was never given to you as a child. This is inner child work on the deepest level. Forgiveness will be imperative. You can get the love and admiration you crave.

Working on your money archetype will be a constant. You will be challenged at home and within your business. You will be challenged by banks and lawyers and accountants. It's ongoing. Lean into that. Allow that truth to resonate. The more you get vulnerable and commit to this lifelong learning, the more quickly your business will thrive and prosper. You can now identify when an old pattern is running and will have the tools to create the shift to get you moving in the direction you want to go.

8

THE POWER OF GRATITUDE

Yeah, I know. Gratitude has become the buzzword of the age.

What do we know about gratitude? Studies show that when we are grateful, we are happier. We have happier emotions. We feel more positive. We have better physical health. Our relationships are better. We feel like there is meaning and purpose in our lives. Seriously, you can't make this up.

How can you start to change your relationship to gratitude? How can you harness the positive and life changing effects?

Hot Tip: *Write down what gratitude means to you.*

I think for some people, gratitude feels fake or contrived. I think other people are more oriented to a lens of gratitude. How we were raised, our cultures and other influences definitely effect our experience of and relationship to gratitude.

But remember, the great thing about our brain is that we can actually change how it filters information. We can learn how to orient it to seek more of what we want, rather than allow what our beliefs and experiences have programmed our brain for. Do you want a big fat gratitude file? Help your RAS by building out opportunities for you to truly appreciate all that you have.

Suspend your resistance here. I want you to really breathe this next part in. I want you to let it seep into your cells and inform your whole body. Allow your mind to think this is dumb or silly or contrived. And do it anyways. Seriously, I haven't been this bossy the whole book, that's how important this practice is.

Start a gratitude practice now. Immediately.

Hot Tip: *The sooner you start this practice, the sooner you will see results. There is always something to be grateful for, even in the darkest of moments. Write it down daily. If you are struggling with this practice, write 2 or 3 things down every hour.*

How do you start a gratitude practice? You might say "Yes, I'm grateful for my apartment, even if it's mouse infested and has leaky, cold windows." The human brain always loves to compare. "Well, it could be worse, I could be homeless."

Reread that paragraph. How does it make you feel? Sit with it. I feel gratitude but I also feel judgement. I feel resentment. I feel "this is crappy, but it could be worse."

Does that sound like your relationship to gratitude? It might be your best start, and that's amazing. Please don't stop. And now consider this statement:

"I am grateful for my apartment. There are a few things I am interested in changing, and yet I love that the stove works and I have a bathroom all to myself."

The mice are still there. So are the leaky windows. Invite the upgrade without deliberately criticizing the lack or the things that are wrong. Because what you are not so subtly saying to yourself is "look, I'm garbage. I can't even afford a nice apartment without mice and leaky windows." And that is just plain old mean to your soul and your spirit and all your hard work.

It's a radical act to work with gratitude without spite. Yes, the world is unfair. Capitalistic greed sucks. Yet this does not diminish the beauty of your life. Do not dismiss the potency of the gifts you have been given or the vibrancy of the beautiful world you inhabit.

How is this landing? Can you feel the difference in your body? Spiteful gratitude (filled with judgement and anger) versus true gratitude? Gratitude that excludes judgement is the goal.

You have a choice here. My invitation to you is to be grateful to things you are really grateful for right now. Without judgement. Without spite. Without greed.

- I am grateful that I can trust my body and pee in the toilet;
- I am grateful that I have a beautiful home;
- I have grateful that I can drink clean water;
- I am grateful I can write;
- I am grateful I have a computer I can write on;
- I am grateful to be home alone to be creative;
- I am grateful I brushed my teeth;
- I am grateful for my amazing husband;
- I am grateful for my children;
- I am grateful I can read.

This is my quick list that I can write right now. Do you see how simple it can be?

And if you are mad that there is fluoride in your water, that's going to affect your result.

If you think "Yeah, I'm grateful I can write but my computer sucks and I really need a new one" -meh.

I am grateful I am alone but actually I wish I wasn't.

That's the quickest way for you to undo your gratitude.

Don't worry. Lots of us are programmed to be pessimists. It protects us from feelings of let-down, failure, and keeps our expectations low.

Start slow. Set the bar low. If this sounds like you, you need to support yourself to allow yourself to feel these winning, grateful feelings. This blossoming of gratitude? I want it to be a lived and felt experience. It's not a time to diminish what you have, all the things you have worked for and created in your life. And please don't complete your gratitude statement with something that is wrong or could use improvement. I mean it. I know, it's your nature, but stop. I'm begging you.

Get so small and tiny here:

- I'm grateful that my anus works;
- I'm grateful that I have beautiful (hair, eyelashes, lips, ears);
- I'm grateful I can smell;
- I'm grateful I can read;
- I'm grateful I have kids;
- I'm grateful I don't have kids;
- I am grateful I am single;
- I'm grateful for the art I have in my bedroom;
- I'm grateful I woke up;
- I'm grateful for coffee;
- I'm grateful for sunshine;
- I'm grateful for rain;

- I'm grateful for my bed.

You see where I am?

To get gratitude to work for you, you must be grateful for what you are writing. And it doesn't have to be big and grandiose. Some days you will be grateful you didn't hurt anyone. Other days you will be grateful for the mysteriousness of life.

Now, how do we find gratitude without judgment? How do we want things to be different while not negating what we have? How do we strive for a better relationship, improved health or wanting more money? Gratitude and wanting change are not mutually exclusive ideals. The act of manifestation and creating positive change never comes from focusing on what we don't have.

Therefore, don't spend your life in denial. Everything you have right now was, at one point, something you wanted, valued, worked for and created. Do you like what you have? It's ok if you want some changes; that's healthy and shows how you are growing and evolving. However, if you are constantly putting down what you have, especially considering how much time, money and energy you had to invest to make this happen, your denial energy will also override all the other ways you are being given gifts.

Your gratitude practice might be "Look at all the love I have for my dog. I appreciate that so much. It's such a blessing. And I would love to share my love with another human being, as a life partner. That would be amazing."

That statement honours that you do know wild, beautiful love. And invites more of it into your life. It becomes an expansion rather than a denial of what you don't have. You can leverage what is already in your life and utilize it to help you create even more.

Viktor Frankl's book, "Man's Search for Meaning", was a book I read when I was 22. I loved it. It changed so many things that I was thinking about. Viktor was a psychiatrist with a clinic in Vienna. He was also Jewish. When the Second World War broke out, he ended up in Auschwitz. And he started to recognize a pattern of survival; it was noticeable. Those people who had meaning and purpose, those who had a "happier" disposition seemed to survive.

> *"But happiness cannot be pursued; it must ensue. One must have a reason to 'be happy.' Once that reason is found, however, one becomes happy automatically."*

He further went on to note:

> *"We who lived in concentration camps can remember the men who walked through the huts comforting others, giving away their last piece of bread. They may have been few in number, but they offer sufficient proof that everything can be taken from a man but one thing: the last of human freedoms—to choose one's own attitude in any given set of circumstances—to choose one's own way."*

How will this help you as a holistic entrepreneur? Gratitude helps you create that choice. Gratitude helps you choose happiness. Once you start pulling the gratitude in, you will bring in even more gratitude. You will see the blessings around you. You will be more resilient. You will experience things as joy and blessings and opportunities instead of just seeing roadblocks, setbacks and failings.

When Michael and I got married, I was already a very happy person. I had troubles; being on call as a midwife was hard, and we had very little money. We were budgeted down to the penny. But we were happy. Yes, blending our families was extremely difficult and we were spending a lot of time with professionals, taking courses, reading and doing lots of things to make these relationships work.

I can't believe it, but Michael and I are happier today. Blissfully, joyfully, honestly happier. How can this be? I really am stunned. I wake up every day and wonder "How can I be even happier?" I am filled with gratitude. And I am convinced that my commitment to being grateful invited more gratitude.

Now, Michael is a different egg. We have had many discussions about his world view. He calls himself a realist. He is always looking for balance. The other side of the coin. He likes to prepare himself for worst case scenarios and has, generally, lower expectations for how things might work out.

We are very different in how we approach the world. We have different experiences of people and how they might show up. You could call me passionately optimistic. Michael would say he is honestly realistic. Why am I telling you all this? Because each of us is still experiencing happiness, joy, and pleasure. We wake up excited to meet the day. I can't wait to see him at the end of a working day. We share and grow and evolve, and have an amazing relationship. Isn't that what everyone wants in a best friend and life partner?

So, what's the secret? Gratitude. You knew it was going there. Once you start this practice you will see how it supports you in ways you could never have imagined.

Hot Tip: *Start doing a gratitude journal every night before you go to bed. When you do this gratitude list before bed, you program your brain and your mind to be subtly focusing on these lovely things through the night. It will relax your brain, soothe your nervous system and sustain you with sweet dreams.*

You also will want to start working with gratitude weekly, especially in the spaces that are difficult for you. I guarantee you are missing all the successes you have.

The easiest way to do this is with Wednesday Wins. Every Wednesday, take five minutes to write down all the things that were successful and that you are grateful for in the past week. It could be work related, parenting, healthier eating or another goal you have for yourself. Start writing down all the ways you were right and good and on track. You don't have to have completed anything. It doesn't need to be gigantic. In fact, it will be more powerful when you celebrate the small, micro steps that you make daily.

You have two simple and effective gratitude practices that will help you get moving, feeling more satisfied and happier. The effects will be noticeable almost immediately. Reprogram your brain, fatten up the RAS file on gratitude and set yourself up for even more joy and bliss. Stick with these practices for at least three months. Then re-evaluate.

Start your gratitude practice today and stay committed. Put a reminder in your phone to write your gratitude before bed. Track your Wednesday Wins. These are small and significant steps that will help your confidence burst forth and help you feel so peaceful and grateful. Your business will start to soar because you cannot help but see all the things you truly can be grateful for.

Affirmations.

Affirmations have gotten a bit of a bad rap recently. I think that's because so many people aren't really sure how to get them to work for them.

Here's the thing; sitting around affirming that you will earn $1,000,000.00 this year isn't going to work. Dreaming about the man of your dreams who is handsome, rich, sexy, gives good back rubs and also loves to eat vegan, same thing. It's not going to happen. Affirmations work well when we pair them with feelings that we can create right now, along with inspired and focused action.

Now, don't get confused here, this doesn't necessarily mean that you need to jump onto Tinder and start dating. That's one idea and might be a step you choose to take to find this dream man. But there are many more ways that you can get them working for you.

How affirmations really work is by:

1. Getting clear on your ask;
2. Identifying and anchoring into the feelings of your ask;
3. Starting to create opportunities to feel those feelings today;
4. Linking some inspired action to the manifestation of that ask;
5. Using phrases and affirmations to support this manifestation which;
6. Helps your brain to see these new opportunities and ways of being.

Let's use an example.

I have been working with my business coach since June of 2020. This was a one-to-one mentorship scenario, it was working well, and I was getting amazing results. I was looking around at what I wanted to support me next and I realized I had a huge gap; I really wanted to be in a MatriarchMind (Mastermind) group. I started doing my research. I was looking at groups all over the world. I didn't care how much they cost; I knew the exact set of skills and opportunities and mentorship I was looking for:

a) I wanted lots of powerful, successful women;

b) I also wanted men in the group (I appreciate their, often very different, points of view);

c) I wanted it to be diverse in its offerings (not just business coaching);

d) I wanted it to be driven around financial success and work/life balance, integrity and some other diversity.

I found a few options, but they weren't perfect. Many of the groups were extremely male oriented. Further, they really focused solely on the business mentorship.

So, I decided I would start one myself. I started dreaming about it. What it would look like and the types of offerings included. I also had just started this manuscript, so I was evaluating out the ins and out of self-publishing or finding a publisher to work with.

And then the solution presented itself. My current coach put together the MatriachMind of my dreams. It included men and women. It focused on your commitment to your business and personal success and it included a publishing deal.

I totally manifested this. I did it through dreaming and getting the feelings in there that I wanted. I was calling out to the multiverse for what I was looking for and I was prepared to do it myself. That's how affirmations and manifestation work.

Let's go back through the steps:

1. My ask was an amazing matriarch mind that was not only centred on financial success;
2. I started imagining it for myself, the feelings, how the meetings would run, the tools we would utilize and how we would feel when we had this amazing, supportive group of awesome humans to learn from;
3. I was leaning heavily on myself and my husband to nourish those feelings. I was starting to write this book and my husband and I are in the middle of starting another business together. This helped me feel the success and growth I wanted and was helping me step out of my comfort zone. We also were spending a lot of time as a couple, strategizing for our new business, doing financial planning and making some other goals for ourselves. (Notice

none of these were related to the business success of Peace Healing Wellness?);

4. My inspired action was to look around at other opportunities. I was prepared to create this scenario for myself if I needed to. I was also in the middle of designing my kitchen and bathrooms renovations. This was an area of our home that I had settled with for a long time. Our bathrooms and kitchen are 1997 beauties. By recognizing that I deserved these beautiful spaces and was taking steps to create them, I was taking inspired action and saying, "look at all the ways I am helping myself to create the life and opportunities I want."

I used goal setting, affirmations, focused and inspired action, and generated the feelings I was looking for. I was able to do this in many different areas of my life and that was how I manifested exactly what I wanted.

Now, here is a secret. You don't need to take any inspired action that relates to your goals. Your inspired action could be drinking water. It could be having an amazing orgasm when you are having sex. It could be going for a walk. Doing a puzzle with your kids.

Hot Tip: *Root what you are affirming for yourself into your daily activities. Allow yourself to see how you can manifest and* *generate these feelings and successes by just being you. The only limitation here is your imagination.*

Another important aspect of affirmations that many people forget about is not switching the affirmations up, and keeping them front and centre in your brain. Remember when we talked about the RAS and how it is only filtering in what it already knows and feels comfortable with? Affirmations can easily become dull background noise without any impact. You want to shake up your RAS and get it focusing on what you are attracting and creating in your life right now. This helps your brain see the opportunities that you are creating by doing this mindset work.

Here's how to keep your affirmations powerful and potent:

1. Keep them focused on what you want, not the how;
2. Place them in your daily life so you see them often (paste words on your water bottle, on the bathroom mirror, or the screen saver of your phone);
3. Change your affirmations (even just one word) every few weeks;
4. Remind yourself of your affirmations before you go to bed;
5. Say your affirmations out loud;
6. Use subliminal affirmation recordings, when appropriate.

Anchor your affirmation "I easily make $10,000 a month in my business" into inspired action. Generate the feelings of making $10,000 a month in your business today. Remind yourself with affirmations of what you are manifesting. Don't jump into the how.

You are telling the multiverse exactly what you want, and you are helping yourself. Affirmations are powerful statements of "Yes, and…" They help our brain to see new opportunities available to us, can help us get creative and see new solutions to a problem or help us feel confident and courageous that we can take a leap.

So, get affirming.

9

BUILDING A RELATIONSHIP WITH YOUR CLIENT

As a holistic entrepreneur, you're here to serve. You definitely want your client to have a fabulous outcome or experience. How do you start to share that fabulous outcome or experience? You have to build a relationship with your client. People buy from people. People buy from an emotional place of feeling. Until you tap into that relationship and understand the needs of your client, you will struggle to share your amazing offer with your potential clients.

Start with figuring out who your client is. What solutions are you offering to that client? What is the transformation you will help your client experience? What are the problems that your clients have that you can help with?

When you are a holistic entrepreneur, you are client focused. You want your client to have success and the best outcome possible.

The very best way to start this process is to develop an Ideal Client framework.

When you are creating your ideal client avatar, you want to keep in mind what their viewpoints are, what their pain points are and what their resistance to change is. How do they spend their time? Where do they go on vacation? What is your Ideal Client passionate about? What do they read? Do they like music?

Here is a checklist to get you started. You need **at least** 50-100 descriptors of your ideal client.

Their Age	Their Sex	Relationships	Children
Where they live (urban, suburban, rural)	Employed? Union? F or P/t	Entrepreneur	Career
Where they vacation	How they spend spare time. Hobbies?	What they do when stressed	What they do for fun
What they spend $ on	What they want to spend $ on but can't	What do they lose sleep over? Greatest fears?	What's their top 3 concerns?
Do they volunteer? Where?	Do they donate $? Where?	What are their political views	Do they love nature?
Do they love technology?	What they do with friends	What they do with their partner	How much $ do they make
Political Views	How they behave when happy	What do they do on the weekend	What they would do if $ and time were no objects
What feelings will they have when they have what you're offering?	Generational values	Education Level	Where do they consume content? (FB, IG, Twitter, newspaper)

As you can see, this is a deep dive into the reality of your client. It will allow you to tailor your offering and communicate directly to your client.

Getting close to your client will help you serve your client. Many holistic entrepreneurs waste their time trying to meet the needs of everyone. Or they have a great solution and are targeting the wrong people. Ideal Client work helps you know exactly who you are serving and how you can help them.

Many holistic entrepreneurs notice that their idea client might look a lot like them. Your ideal client may very well be a manifestation of a person you were a few years ago. Maybe there is something you struggled with for years and found a solution for. That's an asset and wildly compelling. You will be able to directly speak to their fears, their resistance and the solution that they are seeking.

If you are offering elder companionship as a service, you want to know where you should share this offer. Facebook and either a newspaper or seniors centre written ad are probably good choices. Why do I know that? Because the elder's grown daughters are the likely demographic to be on Facebook. It will be important for you to get in front of the daughter because she will most likely be doing a lot of the planning and supports for your client. Alternately, we know that our elders are still accessing the news on TV and reading newspapers. These are also good mediums to share your service.

When you know who your ideal client is, you will know this exact type of information and can tailor your offer to the person you want to serve.

When you start to get really close with your Ideal Client, you are going to realize how to speak to them. You will know what their problems are. What language are they using? What problems do they want solved? What are they worried about?

Hot Tip: *Depending on your business model, you may have more than one ideal client. It's important that you create an avatar for each ideal client. Take the time to do this exercise and even go so far as naming your client. Really anchor in who you serve and visualize them.*

You definitely want to get small and focused here. Are your alarm bells ringing? I hear you. When I first thought about niching down, I panicked.

I burnt out from my midwifery career in a really ugly way. It was painful and I had all they physical symptoms as well. I took a year to just recover and get well. I did a lot of grieving. And then I started Peace Healing Wellness. This was a lovely practice of intuition, energy healing and mentorship. I had spent almost 20 years guiding people and helping them on their healing journey. This seemed like a natural progression and evolution of my skills.

Now, a big part of my practice was not only serving women, but also men and couples. I love working with men and find it incredibly rewarding. I realized that if I really wanted to grow and serve more people, I had to get explicit on what I was offering and to who.

This meant that I had to niche down to who I was serving. My clients are Wild Women. I love the women who think a little out of the box and want to do things their way. I also know how to talk to my ideal client. I know where they hang out. I know what words they like. I know what words they don't like. I know their fears. I know exactly how to get in front of them to allow them to find out if my services are right for them.

I still see men and see lots of couples. It's a beautiful extension of my work. But by niching down, I can help myself stand out to the people I can serve the best. They will find me in this fast-paced world and it's a win/win situation.

Ideal client work is something you should evaluate every 12-18 months. You should definitely re-evaluate this if you change your product of service. This practice of re-evaluation should be assessed with the lens of:

- What worked last year?
- What sales and outcomes did I see?
- What feedback did we get from our clients that help us deliver great solutions?
- What feedback did we receive that shows how and where we need to refocus our work?
- What did we love to share?
- What did our clients love?

- What did our clients hate?
- What goals do we have for our business this upcoming year?
- What target market do we want to serve?
- What financial goals do we want to meet?
- How much time was involved in delivering a specific product or service?
- Do you want to continue with a specific product or service?
- What are the economic or other external forces that might affect your business and client?

Ideal client is about relationship building. You are here to serve your client. You want to help them solve their problems. Using their language, on their platforms and delivering solutions to their issues helps you build that relationship of trust. You client wants to know that you are paying attention. You've taken the time to get to know them and have found a solution that really might work. Spend time with your client in your head every day. Think about things from their point of view. Honour who they are and know what results they are looking for. Getting close to your client and really knowing who they are and what they care about will truly help your business to be successful.

Branding.

Branding is an extension of your ideal client work. Fonts, photos, colours, locations of information, and invoking feelings are powerful ways of communicating with your client.

Your branding should be an extension of what your business is. It is a non-verbal way of communicating to your clients who you are and how you will share your solutions.

There are countless quizzes and colour branding guidelines on the web. I encourage you to seek them out. And I also invite you to frame those in a way that you are communicating to your ideal client. Don't just choose what you love; chose what your client will love too.

Once you know your ideal client, your branding will be an extension of communicating with your client. It helps them know if you are the best solution to their problem.

Hot Tip: *go online and research some brands or companies that are offering similar services to you. Look at their fonts, colours, photos and other elements of their website or communications. Who is their ideal client? Can you tell just from their branding? What things about their branding do you like? What do you dislike?*

You can start to build out your branding based on the feelings you want your client to experience. Are you aspirational? Inspirational? Solutions based? Infusing the energetics of your offerings within your branding is an easy way to communicate non-verbally with your client.

Most research tells us we have about 2/10th of a second to make a first impression. Your branding needs to be a reflection of your values and mission and the transformation that you want your client to experience.

Social Media and Marketing.

This book isn't a step by step "how to". There are lots of other great books and resources out there. However, I will take a quick moment to talk about social media and marketing. But more importantly, I hope you are starting to realize how you want to show up in your business as a successful, holistic entrepreneur. You are getting the flavour, the feeling and the energy behind who you are and how you can help. This is a critical component to successful marketing and your strategy.

Social media and marketing are important aspect of your business. You need to know how to get in front of your audience, establish yourself as the expert and start sharing your knowledge.

Remember, as holistic entrepreneurs, we are here to help people. Don't be afraid to get your face known. That's imposter syndrome, big time. It doesn't serve you or your clients. (Don't worry, I've got you covered with a whole chapter on imposter syndrome.)

Always orient your marketing, public relations and social media in the realm of helping your ideal client. How do you serve your client? How would this product or service help your client? What three things can you help them solve today?

Okay, let's back up. Marketing, public relations and social media. What's the difference?

Marketing: activities you undertake to promote the buying or selling of your service.

Public Relations: the reputation your company or brand has.

Social Media: Platforms that allow people to interact with each other (usually on the internet).

For many years, PR and marketing were often seen and treated as separate and distinctive operations. As a holistic entrepreneur, your marketing and PR will be closely intertwined and may not be particularly well-defined.

Always hold the concept that people buy from people. You want your reputation to be woven into your marketing and vice versa. When you create a positive reputation with your clients and you offer your service or product to them, the more likely they are going to believe that you are the right business for the job. That's how people will buy from you.

Getting Personal.

I had a marketer tell me once that they didn't think personal stories were very professional. I sat with that feedback for a long time. It was an interesting point of view. I can get quite personal on my social media channels. I share my experience and what's happening in my day on my social media platforms.

I had to go back to my ideal client. Did my client want to hear about my life? Were my struggles important to them? Could I build a relationship and more trust with my clients by revealing my own challenges? What about how happy I am? I am married to the man of my dreams and am 100% living the life I want. Is this helpful?

The answer for me is yes. Because I'm selling something personal. I'm offering deep, intimate transformation. I'm offering spiritual teachings. I'm sharing my road map and helping others to realize, create, manifest and sustain the life of their dreams. I need to be honest. I need to practice what I preach. In my case, sharing my trials and tribulations, my vacations, my husband and family is critical to showing up in honesty and integrity with my clients.

But how about if you are a lawyer? Do you want to know about your lawyer's recent vacation? How about the new shoes they bought, where they went on a date or how they are having partner troubles at the law firm? You probably don't really care about any of that stuff. I love my lawyer; she's definitely a friend and I do know lots about her life. However, what I really care about is:

- Is she registered with the law society?
- What are her areas of expertise?
- Can she help me with my concerns (time, acuity, expertise)?

- Cost.

And yeah, ok, my lawyer has some pretty kick ass shoes, but that doesn't determine if I work with her.

Now you can see how ideal client becomes a potent tool in your marketing and PR options. Unless you know those things about your clients, you don't know how to speak to them, where to communicate with them and what's important to them.

You will also need to take some time to build this relationship with you clients. The #1 mistake most people make? They start selling without relationship building. People buy from people. You will need to get your KNOW/LIKE/TRUST (KLT) factor up.

The KLT factor is how you build relationship with your clients and community. Your clients will want to know you. They want to like you and they need to trust you. Do you see why it is so important to share your content regularly? This helps build the relationship.

An easy way to start and increase the KLT factor is through storytelling. Storytelling makes you relatable. Storytelling is one way that we love to learn. It's engaging and there often is a hero aspect within a story. We know who we are rooting for. Or perhaps there is an unexpected twist or surprise ending to your story. You need to be a person. You need to be real. That's how you build that relationship with your clients.

Hot Tip: *Write down a few interesting stories about your life. What difficulties did you overcome to get where you are now? What is a "fun fact" about you? What is a sad experience you had and how has that helped you in your business? How are you the hero of your own story?*

And remember, as holistic practitioners and holistic entrepreneurs, we also know there is a woo factor. You are calling in to you people who resonate with you energetically. They have picked you because you are the person they need to help activate and inspire their healing. You have the medicine, insight and skills they need. Call them in. Manifest them. Stand tall and share what your gifts and offerings are so people can find you. You have a solution that they need. And until you are actively and passionately taking that action to say to the multiverse "here I am, and I want to serve", you will not see the clients that need your solution. You are worth this time and effort and your clients will thank you for it. Consider this work part of your inspired action. It will help you realize that you are capable and able to manifest the people you deeply wish to serve.

Hot Tip: *Take five minutes and do a quick search for the demographic statistics of the different social media platforms. Include*

YouTube, Twitter, Tik Tok, Instagram, Facebook, LinkedIn. Find your demographic and commit to posting there regularly. Just start with 1 or 2 platforms and post at least 1-2 times a week.

Now that you know your ideal client and where they hang out, you get to start working on content. Commit to this work and start sharing who you are and how you can help.

Content Creation and The Expert.

This is probably one of the most challenging parts for holistic entrepreneurs (or any entrepreneur for that matter.) What content are you creating, how do you create it and what do you post? Unless you have a huge staff, big budget and copywriters, you are going to need to devote some time to this part of your business.

Content creation is different than what you are offering in your business. Content creation is about helping you get noticed. It's about sharing what your offerings are. What makes you stand out to your client? What's different and special about you and your offerings?

Always go back to your ideal client avatar. Who are they? What solutions do you have for them? What transformation do you want to help them with? What words do they use? What are their pain points?

The easiest way to start your content creation is to think about and honour what you are an expert in.

Definition of an expert: In a room of average people, what do you know the most about?

This really means average. Just normal humans, standing about chatting. What will you mostly likely know the most about? That's it.

Hot Tip: *Review your expert list from before. Now that you know your ideal client, think how you could weave and share that information into your content. Where is some crossover? What story telling can you weave into what you are posting?*

Remember, you don't need to get creating content about all these things. But when you boost your confidence like this, you start to see all the other ways you can serve your clients and offer a unique way to build a relationship with your client.

Good quality content can be a quote, a blog post, an opinion piece, speaking about something that's going on in the world, a controversial position, a unique solution or a hot tip.

Anything that will help you stand out and be seen and noticed. Social media is a busy place and you only have a short amount of time to make an impression.

Sacred Sexuality and Feminine healing are a small part of my services. But I am extremely passionate about healthy and safe and sacred sexuality. I see that as an important aspect of my service. So, while I might not be teaching sacred sex, I am definitely sharing about sex, bodies, and all the juicy goodness things in that area.

What does this do? This helps my client see me as an expert. It helps my client get to know me more. It builds a relationship and trust between us. My client is thinking "Nadine really might have the solution to help me with my problem."

Even if the only reason some people are following me is because of a certain type of content I'm sharing, that's great. I want them to get something out of what I am sharing. And other business books will tell you that while you want your client to buy from you, that your ideal client also has to have the money to pay you. This is totally true. We are not starting our business as a hobby. Making money is not a dirty word. And I am building relationship with my clients. I am getting street credibility. The more I can help my clients (even the ones who might never purchase something from me), the more likely it is they are going to refer to me. They are going to say to their sister or friend "hey, I totally know someone who is really great. Check her out on IG or

FB. She talks a lot about energy healing and women's sexuality. She might be a fit."

And there is no higher vote of approval than a referral. If you have someone who has a know, like and trust relationship with you and they are sending their loved ones, best friend, mother, or sister to you? This is priceless. That is an amazing endorsement. We all have loved ones. When we share our people with others, we are saying "Hey, I trust you. Take good care of this person, they're precious."

So instead of chasing after your clients and getting people to give you money, focus on providing good quality, targeted information in a way that you client wants to hear from you.

I talk a lot about sex. Sacred feminine. And I share my life, travels and fun with my husband. I am the whole meal deal. I live my life the way I want to and I trust that this inspires others to do the same. I am honest when I nurture my clients. You never know how your information might impact another. Hold faith that the right people will hear your message. Trust that it will land.

Hot Tip: *Staying true to this ideal of positioning yourself as the expert, optimizing a personal relationship with the know, like and trust factor, and sharing good content is the key to a successful PR and marketing strategy.*

Here is my list for what to focus on and prioritize and what to not sweat about:

1. To create beautiful content, you can use a platform like Canva. This is free. You can pay for an upgraded account, but the free platform is excellent;
2. Post regularly on your social media channels. 1-2 times a week is enough;
3. Consistency is key. Show up and get people used to seeing you. You want them to miss you;
4. Start getting people on your email list. Your list is yours. (Social media accounts can be shut down or algorithms can change.);
5. If you have an email list, email once a week;
6. People love a good story. Don't be afraid to be a storyteller;
7. Always focus on nurturing your client;
8. Give great content away for free (You want your client thinking "if they are sharing this great nugget of information, what else do they know?");

9. Run any content through the litmus test "does this resonate with my ideal client?";
10. Plan to nurture your audience for at least 6 months before you try and sell something;
11. Finally, run your content through your core values. Does it align?

Just start there and you will see results. Consistency and patience are key to getting yourself noticed and positioned well with your clients.

Now, what not to do:

1. Don't just rely on free social media platforms (you don't own these platforms and can be locked out at any time or the algorithms can change);
2. Don't spend time or money agonizing about professional photos;
3. Don't get caught up in perfect content. Post regularly, even if it's imperfect;
4. Don't shy away from creating an email list. If your client is on your list, they are yours forever (or until they unsubscribe, whichever comes first);
5. Don't use smarmy tactics like buying followers or gathering emails in nefarious ways;
6. Don't email your list only when you are selling something;
7. Don't spend all your time on creating the perfect course, offering, website or other product. Nurture your potential clients;

8. Don't worry about spending money on ads. Ads can be great, but great free content will get you a following really quickly too;
9. Don't be afraid of being spicy or controversial, as long as it's honest and true for you.

The absolutely best way to get in front of your clients?

Spend your time creating a relationship.

Nurture your clients.

Share with them.

Provide great content.

Help them solve their problems.

Post consistently.

I wish someone had broken this down for me. I was so overwhelmed. I am an amazing entrepreneur, but I was working in a whole new landscape. Follow the steps above and just start. You can take more courses and training as you go. You might be able to hire someone. But the most important thing is to nurture your clients and be consistent. Use your core values and stay true to your ideal client. You are here to help.

That's all you need to do to start. It's simple and straightforward. Consistency is key. Love your client up and create that amazing relationship.

10

IMPOSTER SYNDROME

Imposter syndrome can be one of the most debilitating aspect of being a holistic entrepreneur. I believe that imposter syndrome might be even more difficult when you are a holistic entrepreneur. How is it different? Many entrepreneurs are heavily focused on money, sales and other outward symbols of success and status. A holistic entrepreneur is focused on those things and on delivering an incredible service or experience. They care that their clients are happy. They want to deliver top notch information. That can leave us paralyzed with anxiety, perfectionist behaviours, performance issues, "I'll be ready when" narratives, and other negative beliefs and self-talk that makes it really hard to get out there.

What exactly is Imposter Syndrome?

> " Impostor syndrome is a psychological pattern in which an individual doubts their skills, talents or accomplishments and has a persistent internalized fear of being exposed as a "fraud". Despite external evidence of their competence, those experiencing this phenomenon remain convinced that they are frauds, and do not deserve all they have achieved." [1]

Sound familiar? Do you have imposter syndrome? Do you think "oh maybe I got here from luck or was in the right place at the right time." Those are deeply ingrained beliefs and thoughts in people who are experiencing imposter syndrome and it is especially prominent in women.

Almost everyone experiences Imposter Syndrome at one time or another. It can rear its ugly head when we are given promotions, more responsibility, or make a sudden leap in earned income. "Who am I to lead, teach, manage all these people or make this much money?"

Healing Imposter Syndrome.

How do we work with Imposter Syndrome? Well, the first thing to remember is that feelings and thoughts are not facts. Even though you might think you aren't ready or are feeling like a fraud, take a few deep breaths and create some space between those thoughts and feelings and yourself. We are often not even aware of all the things we are saying to ourselves. When we get quiet and realize we are not just a bundle of thoughts and feelings, we can step back and evaluate what's going on and how we want to deal with it. This is an invitation to create choice. That's all we are doing here. Find a way to interrupt the negative feedback loop. Create a choice point and then decide how you want to move to the next step and deal with the feelings you are having.

Hot Tip: *Set the timer on your phone for one minute. Write down your fears or beliefs of how you are not good enough and not ready to make these offerings. And believe me, one minute is MORE than enough!*

It's a powerful tool when you can start to recognize your negative self-talk and beliefs. You now can choose to keep them or create and practice an interruption process.

Every time you have an unwanted feeling or belief or thought run through your head, I would ask you to stop. Pick the thought up. Let it be real and resonate within you. Can you feel it? Where is it living in your body? What are the feelings here? What pains do you get? Headache? Anxiety? Stomach pains? Diarrhea? Get intimate with these feelings and sensations. Once you start tuning in here you will be amazed at all the ways your body is telling you "Alert! Alert!" These feelings, thoughts and bodily sensations are potent signals for you to understand because you now have the information about what's going on, how you are feeling and how it might be affecting you. You now get to decide how to respond to all this information.

Hot Tip: *You may want to go back here to the chapter on Chakras. Review the information your body might be giving you with different feelings, thoughts and various physical sensations.*

Now you might have some awareness of the feelings and thoughts and how they are showing up for you when you experience imposter syndrome. You have sat with them and let the sensations be real. Do not suppress them. Don't pretend they are not there. Give them some space. Don't start looking for stories or information that will confirm this thought or opinion. Just let all the sensations be.

Now, in your mind I want you to place the feeling, thought or idea on a chair in front of you. It might look like you or can take on any type of symbolism you might want. Maybe it has a colour or is a cloud. Perhaps it looks like a frog. Just allow it to be there. Acknowledge it. See it fully. See yourself sitting across from it. Take a few deep breaths.

Now I want you to thank it. Thank it for all they ways it tried to help you. Thank it for trying to protect you from failure, from feeling shame, embarrassment or any other terrible experience you might have had. You are not stupid. You didn't pick up these thoughts and feelings to keep yourself stuck and small. These were probably coping measures that you developed in response to stressful experiences and situations. Celebrate that. Affirm to yourself "this was the best I could do at the time." It was a good solution and helped you get where you are today. Thank you.

Once you have felt that gratitude, I want you to say "I am also grateful that you are here and have woken me up to how I am holding myself back. I see how this no longer serves me. Thank you for being that reminder. Now I know when I am feeling this way, I am being given an amazing clue. Something is going on here that I can choose to address. This is amazing. Look what self-awareness I now have. Thank you for this gift of knowing. Thank you."

Creating space between those negative thoughts and feelings now allows you to think about what thought and feeling you would like to cultivate. Think about this. Is it joy? Creativity? More love? Confidence? Anchor into ways that you have felt those feelings and thoughts in the past and give yourself permission to move into these new ways of being. Until you have a technique to create space between your thoughts, feelings and your whole self, you will continue to run on autopilot.

Sound hokey? Maybe. And I know this works. It takes practice and dedication. And you might have a million thoughts running through your head every day that you have no idea are there. Or maybe you just have a few. It really doesn't matter. We are all learning and growing and evolving. Try this out for a month. See if you can take that 3-5 minutes to do the exercise above. I guarantee if you start working with your fears and beliefs, if you actually make space at the table for them and allow them to be real, you will actually be able to change them and work with them rather than against them.

Another easy way to start to shift your feelings of imposter syndrome is to leverage another time in your life when you also felt not good enough/not ready and then were proven wrong.

For example, let's say you were voted team captain for your grade 6 volleyball team. EEK. You probably had never been captain of a volleyball team before. What the heck? You don't know what to do. You aren't really sure what the job of a captain is. But how did it work out? Can you laugh at some of the mistakes you made? How did you team support you? Did you have a teacher that guided you? Maybe your mom or dad or older sibling was able to help. Recognizing that you have been in this situation before and anchoring to it is one way of starting to rewire the brain and quiet it down. "Shh little brain, yes I know you're worried about this and remember that time we….?"

Utilizing the past experiences that you had will help you move through those feelings of Imposter Syndrome more quickly. And make no mistake, it takes practice, commitment and vulnerability. I know you already have those qualities because you're a holistic entrepreneur.

If you are actively working with the exercises above, you will create a small space between the torrent of thoughts and feelings you have at any moment and yourself, as a whole and amazing human. Keep practicing.

Imposter Syndrome and the Chakras.

Our subconscious brain runs the show 95% of the time. 95%. That means that you are walking around, running on autopilot for most of your life. Your beliefs, experiences, RAS and habits are making almost all of your decisions for you.

Let's run through some of the ways I have seen people experience their negative beliefs and imposter syndrome:

- Extreme anxiety;
- Procrastination;
- Worrying about things you can't control;
- You're snapping at your kids and your partner;
- Unhappy relationships;
- Sabotage;
- Can never achieve their goals;
- Perfectionism;
- Not applying for the job or promotion.

And some of the physical symptoms:

- Diarrhea;
- Allergies;
- Food sensitivities;
- Constipation;
- Stress related illnesses;
- Headaches;
- Insomnia;
- Blood sugar issues;
- Thyroid imbalances (especially in women);
- Menstrual issues;
- Exhaustion.

The list goes on and on.

If Imposter Syndrome is living in your 2nd chakra, you will suffer from abundance issues. You will jump from project to project and suffer from "Oh, Shiny" syndrome, when you move from one idea to another all the time because it's better, faster, cooler and more awesome than you last great idea. You will feel like a victim and chaos will surround you and be present in your life.

If Imposter Syndrome is living in your 3rd chakra, you will procrastinate. You will suffer with perfectionism because something is either right or it's not. You will seek constant reassurance and reinforcement from your clients, your partner and your community. You might come across as arrogant or haughty. You might not be able to take constructive criticism. You will need a lot of adoration before you can take the next steps.

Finally, sometimes Imposter Syndrome can be found in your 5th Chakra. If it's showing up here, it will look like needing to have everything all figured out. You will need evidence that things are correct. You will want to have your entire course, product, offering completely mapped out, right down to the paper you write on and the font you are using. Creativity will be blocked. You will feel lonely and unable to ask for help. You will think that no one gets you.

Hot Tip: *Were you able to identify which chakra your Imposter Syndrome might be living in? Do you see how you could now interrupt the patterns that are running there and start to change your thoughts, behaviours or beliefs and get a different result? Go back to review the section on the chakras for some more ideas on how you can support yourself right now with any issues you might be experiencing.*

We have ample evidence of the mind/body connection. Certainly, don't just chalk up your physical health to your emotional health. Pop in to see your healthcare provider and get the tests to rule out any physical issues. However, if you continue to downplay the role your emotional well-being and thoughts have on you, you are missing a huge component to your overall health and wellbeing. This is a major opportunity and invitation for you to have the life of your dreams right now.

Replacing Feelings of Imposter Syndrome.

You now have two incredible tools to help you interrupt the pattern of negative self- talk and beliefs. You can start to recognize when unsupportive beliefs and emotions are running the show. What do you want to replace those thoughts and feelings with? You have to know. And if you don't know, you have to have an idea. It's ok if it's not perfect but you definitely must replace them, or the old ways will just take over. Go back to your personal core values. Go back to your embodiment board. Take a look and see what feelings you want to create and bring more of into your life. Breathe it in. Now commit to bringing those positive emotions into your feelings around imposter syndrome and anchor into the feelings you do want.

The amount of energy and mental gymnastics it takes to resist negative feelings and thoughts is gigantic. Imagine if, instead of being plagued with bad dreams, insomnia, interfering thoughts that poke into your head at unwanted times, obsessive thoughts, lack of concentration and a whole host of other unwanted behaviours jumping into your mind, how it might feel if you actually knew and believed you were good enough? When you actively take control of your mind, your habits and your feelings, suddenly you can leverage them for success, fun teaching moments and nuggets of wisdom. You are a whole human being with an amazing set of skills and life experiences. This practice helps you integrate all of those learnings to make you a more whole person instead of fragments and compartments of you.

Ok, the bad news. If you don't create time to work with these things, they become this nefarious wafting of negative beliefs and self-talk that pours through your body. The energy undermines you in your self-confidence, in your feelings of worthiness and in your creativity. Stuffing it down means that it is directing your life in ways that you may have no awareness of. You may be completely unconscious about all the ways these feelings and beliefs are influencing your behaviour and even the choices and opportunities you see available to you. Money issues, attracting clients, sharing your product, your relationship and even sex. Each of these areas are being impacted.

Finally, (and this is some really good news), it gets easier. Once you implement a process and system to get out of these negative beliefs and self-talk, you will more quickly recognize it when they show up. You will have fewer and fewer damaging beliefs running your life. You will be able to stop the brain train running down the rabbit hole and turn those moments into potent choice points to get the results you want. I have been doing this work for over 20 years and shared it with thousands of my clients. Give it a real shot and you will see results.

Imposter Syndrome and the Wounded Healer Archetype.

Feelings of imposter syndrome is also another way that the wounded healer archetype might show up for you. If the wounded healer archetype is running, you will definitely think you are not good enough. "See, I'm not healed, how could I heal anyone else?"

As a healer, you know you don't heal people. You inspire healing. You hold up a mirror. You shine a flashlight. All of these things are beautiful and potent ways that we support others to find their peace and healing journey. And healing, like entrepreneurship, is a journey, not a destination. Do you agree?

You only need to be one step ahead of your client. One. You only need to know a little bit more. And if you are trust the power of manifestation and believe that the people you are meant to work with will find you, then you know that you have the words, insight and skills to inspire that healing journey in your clients.

Hot Tip: *Can you sit with the paragraph above? I want you to reread it and breathe it in. Does it feel disingenuous? Out of integrity? Or does it feel compassionate, to yourself and your clients? Jot down what expectations you place on yourself when it comes to serving your clients and your business.*

You are here to serve and will stand in that space with integrity. You will honour your client's journey and your own journey. Take some time to examine your beliefs and feelings around the wounded healer issue. It is very likely to be a considerable cause of your imposter syndrome.

Finally go back to your Expert Status list. What are you an expert at? Review this list. Document all the ways you are excellent for this job. Write it down. Journal about it before you go to bed. Ask your partner to tell you all the ways you're perfect for this position. If you are a normal human (and I am assuming you are), then you probably suffer from the problem of focusing on your lack. You miss your wins. You gloss over your successes and feel like your faults are magnified. I invite you to take deliberate and focused action right now. Interrupt this cultural pattern of duplicity and deprecation. It doesn't serve you, your family or your business.

Everyone's a Critic.

We live in a public world. Social media is a mainstay for most of our lives. We all know that people are posting their wins and successes, and deep down we are wondering if they really do have it all and we are failing.

This is normal human behaviour. You have to snug into this space. You can know in your mind that what is happening on social media isn't the whole story, and yet you can still allow yourself to feel in your belly the wounding and nervousness and wondering if you really are behind in the game of life. (You aren't).

You may choose to not generate and share your content on social media. Building your business does not mean you have to be in this space. However, if you are on social media, you know the judgement of the crowd might come down on you next.

How do you want to show up to this public space? The most important pieces as a holistic entrepreneur are confidence and integrity. You have to have enough confidence to get yourself out there. It can be really scary. And you have to have the integrity to stand in your truth, which includes honouring when you are wrong, when you may have trespassed against someone or didn't have all the information.

Everyone wants to be liked. Everyone wants to be seen for their uniqueness and value and cool little awesomeness.

Hot Tip: *I invite you to build a relationship with some competing interests when considering how you want to be visible in your business.*

1. *We all have a need to fit in and be liked.*
2. *How is your need to fit in and be liked potentially in conflict with your honesty and integrity when showing up in your business?*
3. *Find some balance here by recognizing that your vulnerability and honesty are huge opportunities for you to stand out to your ideal client, and people might not like you for this.*

For the majority of the holistic entrepreneurs I have worked with, fear of visibility holds them back the most. They aren't sure what they are offering. They know they might appear a little fringe. They know some people will take advantage of their good nature. People won't agree with them. And worst of all, what if they harm someone?

You will mess up. You will be judged. You already have messed up. Some people already are judging you. This is inescapable in our current humanity. Can you feel how it still lives in your body? Where does this land for you?

Evaluate your procrastination pathway. Is fear holding you back from being visible? Or is it not a priority?

I have witnessed so many of the people who came out of Healer's Training be paralyzed by the criticism and judgement. What's really holding them back? Criticism and judgement of themselves. Believing they are not good enough. Imposter Syndrome. If you are playing small, not sharing your gifts, minimizing the solutions you have or not sharing yourself, you are definitely holding onto that energetic space.

The phrase "haters gonna hate" is true. It will always be true. Expect that some people won't resonate with you and won't like what you do. I hear you, you just said in your head, "yeah, I know that." But do you?

Unless you are willing to face those fears and do the thing anyways, I would guess that fear and judgement are still playing huge roles in your brain. Fear and judgement are Feelings of imposter syndrome are dictating how you are living your life.

This also relates back to your ideal client. Remember when you wrote down all the amazing things about the people you wanted to serve? Are you still pushing back on that idea? That's scarcity mindset. You're sitting there thinking "Energy healing is for everyone" Or "Aromatherapy is an effective healing tool and should be accessible to all" You're not wrong. But you're also not right. By holding on so tight to this scarcity mindset (I know, you think it's expansive, stick with me and I will tell you why it's not), you are inviting people to criticize you. You are trying to speak to everyone, so your information is diluted. You are going to say the right thing to the wrong person. Or you will say the wrong thing to the right person.

I do not dilute the fact that the work I share, and the journey I go on with people, is deeply spiritual. Every single client that I have seen knows this. They know this is my lens. They know that I will be bringing that into their experience with me. I work with Christian's, atheists, and all other types of people with diverse spirituality. But no one has been upset with this, because it's up front. I don't need to hide it. Come or don't. I may be a fit or I might not. Your personal beliefs and spirituality will inform part of our time together.

Until you too can stand firmly into that space and know who you are speaking too, the risk of pissing someone off and getting into a sticky conversation that you don't want to have is high. You are increasing your odds of judgement and negative feedback. And you will probably trigger the Imposter Syndrome feelings that are living inside of you.

If being polarizing and challenging people is part of your mission and your medicine, I want you to go for it. But if it's not, I would encourage you to be forthright on what you're offering and to whom.

If being polarizing is not an important part of the work you do, take yourself out of it. You don't need to convince anyone. As holistic entrepreneurs, we are here to serve. Someone else may be better suited to serve that client's needs. Let that client go and to find the experience they want. Then you can create more space and get into the business of serving the clients that want you.

And the scarcity, are you seeing it? The more tightly we grasp onto the idea that you are here to serve and help and give solutions to everyone, the more quickly no one is sure if you're right for them. Get so clear and sparkly on your mission and values that no one is even looking twice at you if you're not right for them. Let your clients know how you are so perfect for them. Stay committed to what your solutions are and how you are perfect for your ideal client. The criticism you will face will hurt less when you focus more on who you are and why you are doing it.

11

MENTORSHIP AND THE PERPETUAL STUDENT

Entrepreneurship can be lonely. You may not have a lot of staff or employees. Or you might have a lot of people working with you. Either way, find a community of awesome humans and surround yourself with people who are smarter, more successful and where you want to be. This may sound counter-intuitive, but good mentors and leaders will build you up. They want you to be successful. This is back to the value of interdependence and win/win scenarios. No woman is an island. You most definitely want to get out and hang out with people who know more than you. Seek this out relentlessly. Always have a circle of people around you who will push you, call you out on your bullshit, and also see you for the shining and brilliant star you are.

Mentors will also stretch you. They want you to reach higher and further. When you have great mentors around you, you realize their humanity. It suddenly does become possible for you because you know they are just a beautiful human who was once where you were. Your journeys might have been a little different, yet ultimately, we are all simple humans, just doing the best that we can in our own lives.

When I started this latest holistic entrepreneur journey, I was looking around me for other women who were smart, successful and thriving in the holistic, spiritual and wellness sphere. My options were lacking. There is a void in the wellness and healing industry. Many healers struggle to bridge the gap between providing an essential service and charging for it. I had struggled there too. I didn't want to be stuck in that churn of working hard, honing my skills, providing amazing service and sharing it with the most people possible, all while not being properly remunerated.

I looked at my circle and didn't see what I wanted. So, I hit the internet. There are tons of amazing coaches out there. And because I am holistic and spiritual and all that juicy woo-woo, I trusted that the right person would be there. I would find them, and they would find me.

Well, you know how that story ends. I ended up on a free group session where this business coach was speaking about passive income. Ok, a) I wasn't totally sure what that was (is this about rental properties?) and b) I had never heard of her in my life.

I immediately stalked her. Found her webpage and joined her free group. She was not woo-woo at all. I sat, listened andwatched what was happening. And I loved her. She was super smart and had all the business tools that I was lacking. I was in.

I signed up for one of her courses. After the first day, I knew I had to ask about private, 1 to 1 coaching. I fired off an email and had a good cry. You see, she only works with a very few, select clients and I desperately wanted to be one. I knew that I had to up-level my game, for myself and for my clients. I have a lot of good stuff to offer and playing small was serving no one.

You guessed it; she took me. It's been an incredible journey. I have to take a lot of responsibility. I have to watch and learn and grow. I need to get uncomfortable. Unless you have someone smarter, wiser, savvier, wealthier and more successful around you, you probably won't stretch yourself. You need to set the bar high and reach for it.

This is where a lot of people get stuck. They are super threatened by another person's success. They don't see the win/win or no-go energy. They think this person is better than them. They think we are fighting for the same clients, have a lack mindset or other set of beliefs and values that doesn't serve them. If this sounds like you, I am going to challenge you to get out of your ego and into your heart. Until you can see another person as brilliant, wise, skilled and able to teach you, you will always be in conflict and competition. Those energies don't really serve us as holistic entrepreneurs. Even in the most difficult of times, recognizing the shortfalls we have is vital to our growth, our offerings and our personal development.

Now, you may have had a terrible experience with a coach or leader or healer. That's totally valid. And now you know why your core values are so important. When you understand your chakras, and how those might show up in collapse, you help yourself identify what needs are not being met. You know your triggers. You know your heart. And until you are able to honestly ask for help, be challenged and know that there are gaps in your knowledge that someone else can help with, you will continue to struggle and underperform.

For women in particular, there is no more powerful and potent mentor than another powerful and potent woman. Most women are not taught leadership and mentorship. Some of us are not inherent teachers. But understand that until we take the time and make the effort to fill and heal that gap within our community, we will continue to flounder within the world we live in. Seek out people who are different. Find a powerful woman mentor. They have had different life experiences, knowledge and have amazing things they can share with you.

I had a client ask me "why did you hire a coach who wasn't into energy and woo-woo and all that good stuff?". My answer? "Because I am already really good at that." I don't need someone to stroke my ego and have the confirmation bias that I am good at energy healing and mentorship, reinforce the "build it and they will come" energetic baloney, or other spiritual and woo type business philosophies. I wanted ethical, strong, and effective skills and techniques that I could implement. I can make them unique to me and see success in my business. She was the right woman for the job.

I was taught the power of women mentorship as a young and eager apprentice midwife. Ok, a quick little background here. When I started down the midwifery pathway, midwives had just become registered healthcare professionals in the province I live in. There was no funding for the essential services we provided. Midwives did not have hospital privileges. We were some pretty fierce cowgirls. We were catching babies in the middle of the Prairies with little support from our doctors, hospitals, emergency services teams or even the laboratory.

I was mentored by two beautiful, smart and courageous women. They each practiced midwifery a little differently and were quick to share their opinions. These women deeply wished to serve the families that came to them for care. They were firmly centred on the rights of women and birthing people. They inspired me in so many ways.

And the opportunity? Well, it was incredible. Because we were so excluded in the healthcare community, we depended on ourselves. These midwives expected me to study hard and practice my skills. I was terrified of IV's and had to desensitise myself by hanging photocopied photos of IV's in arms all over my kitchen cupboards. Also, did you know if you have a good friend, they will let you poke around to try and find a vein in their arm, all in the name of getting me proficient in starting an IV? Anyways, I digress. Ultimately, I was positioned to be a key part of the team. I had to understand all of the equipment and set it up properly and safely. I had to follow directions and orders that I may or may not have fully understood. I had to have the confidence in myself and my team that we could deal with any situation that might arise. We all had to trust the team and lean on each other for strength if things got hard. I was treated as a valued and important member of the team, even though my knowledge and skill set were limited. The way we were each valued, and the honouring of the strengths and weakness we individually brought to the table, was a lifelong gift and taught me the true meaning of teamwork.

I also had the distinct privilege of working in a profession that is peopled almost entirely by women. We are feisty and smart and keen and devoted and wise. Midwives are an incredible group of women. Until you find this circle, you will underestimate the power and support you can experience for yourself and offer to others. Find a mastermind, a mentorship program, a course or community of women. Make sure some of them are more "successful" than you. And honour how you might be more "successful" than them. This circle of women will be one of the most supportive things you can do and will help you grow well beyond your wildest dreams.

Perpetual Student Mindset.

Another important aspect of getting over imposter syndrome is continued learning. If you can adopt a mindset of perpetual student, you will be more open to learning and growth. You won't feel threatened when you realize there is more to learn, or when you realize there is a deficiency in your knowledge. And you might be arguing with me here, thinking "I'm not threatened." Unless you can name at least three other women that are doing something you want to be doing, and are doing it more successfully than you, you're still in your comfort zone.

- How many books do you read in a year?
- Do you take courses regularly -and not about business or your profession, but about something fun or creative?
- Do you travel somewhere new at least once a year?
- Do you seek out others who know more than you in your field?
- Do you actively cultivate real relationships with people who are different from you?
- When was the last time you hit up a different grocery store or coffee shop?
- Are you hanging around with people who are of the same race, religion or socio-economic background?

Unless you are making a conscious effort to challenge your beliefs, your world view and expand your knowledge base, you are suffering from confirmation bias.

> "Confirmation bias is the tendency to search for, interpret, favor, and recall information in a way that confirms or supports one's prior beliefs or values. People tend to unconsciously select information that supports their views but ignoring non-supportive information."[1]

When we don't have the perpetual student mindset, we create a story in our heads that we are "set up", or that we already know the answers. Even if you are not conscious of these beliefs or feelings, until you are actively seeking out alternatives, different points of view and new ideas, you will snug back into the Reticular Activation System of filing and filtering in only that which meets your brain's predetermined ideas. Once you adopt this perpetual student mindset, you will see the world through a whole new lens. You won't have to be right. Others automatically become a teacher. And so do you.

Hot Tip: *Write down three people that inspire you and you want to learn from. Figure out a way to be more engaged with them. Buy their book, take their workshop or follow them on social media. Now choose one person who is really different than you are, but you have a little fascination about them. Buy their book or find another way to learn from them.*

Perpetual student mindset is a radical act of compassion. When you actively engage in this energy, your ego will soften. It suddenly becomes ok to be wrong. Your heart and mind are safe and protected. It's ok to ask questions. You won't look stupid. And you can safely open your mouth to share something or respond to a request on social media with your answer. Suddenly either/or thinking can fade away and you can blissfully enjoy the shades of grey.

Another important component of this perpetual student mindset is challenging ourselves to have relationships with others that are different than us. When we insulate ourselves within our own weird little worlds, talking to the same people who have the same ideas as our own, we miss the incredible wisdom and experiences of other people. We miss an important lens of new insights and information because we are only letting in what our little brains already know and like.

Finally, I want you to think about how being a perpetual student helps you build resiliency, banishes imposter syndrome and anchors you within yourself as a proud, capable and a whole human doing the best that you can.

When you are truly able to listen, witness, ask, hear and understand another point of view, you are doing two things:

1. You are honouring the person in front of you as a whole being, listening to them without judgement and seeing them as whole and complete;

2. You will be able to take in information and flesh out your ideas and ideals more fully. You might learn something.

Once you can get really good at holding two different points of view (or more) in your mind, and not feel threatened or attacked, you will strengthen your commitment to your values, your own knowing and your well-being.

This perpetual student lens gives you a whole other superpower that you can lean into. You will be confident in your decisions and will create space for it to be ok if you fail. You can expand and change and adapt and continue to grow your business. This mindset will help you in ways you might not see right away, but trust me, the ride is wild and fun and darn it, the world is interesting! Get out there and experience it.

12

QUICK STEPS FOR GETTING SOME WINS TODAY

This is basically the "too long didn't read" section of the book. If you are look for quick, easy solutions that you can implement today, keep reading.

Get a routine. Get one now. Start your day off with some basic things to set you up for success.

Here's my morning routine:

Get up around 6 am;

Coffee with my husband, check in, chat about our day;

Journal any dreams, ideas, thoughts;

Read the news and articles (no Facebook or Instagram);

Pick a word for the day;

Pick a tarot card for the day;

Review my schedule (including time blocking my day for tasks; I do the hard ones first);

Get dressed, breakfast etc.

My routine is pretty simple. I stick to it. I don't walk or exercise. I don't meditate first thing. No matter what your routine is find something and do things that will support you for a successful day.

I almost always meditate in the afternoon. Or nap. It's usually just for 5-10 minutes but either way I look forward to the rest and recharge. Take the time to find a routine that works for you. It's doesn't have to be super regimented and stressful but create a supportive routine. You will feel so much better when you do.

Feeling emotional? Work with your sense of smell.

You read that right. The sense of smell is a strong and potent part of our brains. The limbic system of your brain plays a huge role in your emotions, your memory and can influence your behaviour. Working with smell is an easy way to influence the limbic system, change up how you are feeling, anchor memories, and change your behaviour.

Here are some easy suggestions that most people will have in their homes so you can start shifting now.

You could also buy a plant or essential oils if that was something you wanted to work with.

Citrus (orange, grapefruit, lemon and lime) = mood enhancers, happiness, bright and light feelings.

Coffee = warmth, joy, cozy (these are my associations. Think of what yours might be).

Lavender = calm, relaxed, nurtured.

Rose = loved, warmth, surrounded by loved ones.

Cedarwood = courageous, grounded.

Fir or Pine Trees = earthy, worthy, safe.

Geranium = powerful relaxant, hormone balancing.

Clove = warm, open, inviting.

Cinnamon = spicy, joyful, connected.

This is a quick example of a few items that you could work with. Go buy yourself flowers and breathe them in. Make a cup of coffee or tea. Pop into your spice cupboard and sniff around.

Find the smells around you to get you shifted, quickly and efficiently, out of those bad moods. Maybe you have had a bad call with a client. Or you had to send a crappy email. Take two minutes to find something that you love to smell and breathe it in. The act of a few deep breaths and this gorgeous new scent will ground you and help you move forward. You will feel so much better.

Now, wondering if this is a bit of a bypass? Are you side stepping some work or issues that you might need to dive into and just trying to find a quick and easy work around? Maybe. So, here's the thing. If a memory or trauma comes up and it's "not a good time", use the smells around you to lift your mood and shift your state so you can remain focused. Having done that, if the issue that was coming up for you is deep, painful and traumatizing, you may want to put some attention here and work on that issue. Consider finding a good therapist, energy healer, naturopath, physician or other healthcare provider. This is just another opportunity for you to heal and grow. Whatever is holding you back is something that you can find good help and support for. Carve time out for it in your day. You might even need to schedule it into your calendar. Otherwise, these thoughts and memories are going to creep in and keep popping up.

Your painful memories and experiences are not trying to disrupt your flow and make you feel like you're are crazy or broken. They are saying "we need help". Make sure to create space for that. When these memories and traumas are asking for your attention, you deserve all that care and attention. If you don't create space for this work, you may struggle with disturbed sleep, anxiety, depression, or other stress related symptoms. This is going to deeply impact your effectiveness. And you most definitely deserve some peace and healing.

Wednesday Wins.

You should be tracking your wins, weekly. Write down all the ways you had success in the previous week. From the smallest ones (got my kids to school on time every day this week) to the biggest (closed a $1,000,000.00 deal.)

All of your wins should be tracked. Remember, you are reprogramming your brain to help you see all the ways you are successful and amazing. Believe me, you are missing them. Track now and do it weekly. Put a reminder with an alert in your calendar. Write your wins in a journal and leverage your successes.

Gratitude.

Get in the habit of doing non-judgemental gratitude statements before you go to bed. (Head back to the gratitude chapter to find out more.)

When you reprogramme your brain to be focused on gratitude, and do this before you go to bed, you will be amazed at how these feelings and truths float through your mind, body and soul as you are in dreamland. I'm convinced you will sleep better too. This is especially true for women, who are often plagued with thoughts and worries about the kids, their business, the looming deadline, oh, and what was I supposed to bring to family dinner on Friday?

You also must write it down. Writing anchors the gratitude in your mind and it also becomes a physical act within the body. Explore all the different ways you can experience and feel gratitude: in the body, reading it, a sound, a sight or a smell. The more opportunities you give yourself to feel and explore gratitude, the easier it will be for you to know it.

Play.

You must play. Every, single day. Yep. I'm totally serious. And I guarantee you are not playing enough right now. You might take a break; you might scroll on social media. Maybe you read. You might get down on the floor and play with your kids. But that's not play. That's distraction, responsibility and "doing the right thing".

Play looks like:

- Having a bubble bath with candles, prosecco and just soaking;
- Taking a dance break to your favourite song from when you were a kid (I Want Your Sex by George Michael is a favourite right now);
- Going for a walk outside (even just 10 minutes) and checking out the trees or birds (not walking the dog or listening to a podcast);
- Sketching in your journal for fun;
- Cooking for joy and pleasure ;
- Watch your favourite TV show (but just 1 episode. Binging is zoning out.);
- Practice your handstands;
- Lay in corpse pose for 5 minutes;
- Put on your favourite wild lipstick;
- Laugh, a lot, long and hard;
- Chat with a girlfriend on the phone for a few minutes;

- Stand on the front porch and listen to the birds singing or watch the sunrise;
- Text your partner that you want to have sex later and arrange a sex date. Get excited about it;
- Play a musical instrument (even just for 5 minutes);
- Read something just for fun;
- I always have fresh cut flowers in my house. They make me happy;
- Buy a plant and talk to it. Name it. (I have a plant named Nadine.) Plants are not judgemental and will be happy to listen to you;
- Go have a fire. Outside or in your fireplace. Just gaze at it;
- Go sledding or skating;
- Go surfing or swimming;
- Sit at a beach or beside a river or stream, throw rocks in;
- Sing loudly;
- Spend some time in sacred naked;
- Masturbate.

How do you know if you are playing? The only reason for your action is for your pure and unbound pleasure. There is no secondary gain, no "I really should practice my handstands" or other story attached to it.

Dancing and movement are some of the best forms of play. It frees us up, gets our bodies moving, and invites silliness into the space. Singing, joy, and playfulness brings us back into our bodies. If you are dancing all weird and wildly, laughing, head thrown back, you are in the wonderous pleasure and moment of your life.

Hot tip: *write down a quick list of things you can do to play. Get super creative here and really allow yourself to be free and unencumbered. When you get bored of your go-to ways, you will have a list that you can grab and pick something from. Or, even more playful, close your eyes and let your finger land on the thing you will do. Get playing.*

Ok, so I actually love that you're here. If you start working with one or two of these suggestions right now and get consistent with them, you will see improvements. Immediately. Your mood will be better, you will feel more energized, you will be happier and feel more motivation to get those hard things done.

You don't need to do them all. You don't need 100% improvement. All we are looking for is just 1% improvement every day. Small, simple and tiny. Because remember, you are awesome. You are doing good work. The world needs you. Trust that you are amazing and recognize that you have the ability to grow and change and improve your life, one tiny behaviour at a time.

13

CHARGING FOR YOUR SERVICES

Many holistic entrepreneurs struggle with the pricing of their services. They are constantly evaluating their costs. They may not be paying themselves enough.

If you are in the healing arts world, this aspect of your business might give you a lot of troubles. What is particularly interesting, and I hope you noticed, is that I have not include this chapter in the Money Magic section of the book. Why? Because until you evaluate your own relationship with money, you will not be able to read this section and actually apply it successfully to your life. You must work with non-judgemental gratitude. You have to get your core values down and you need identify your Money Archetype wounding and mentality. These will be ongoing learnings and you will always find new ways to trip yourself up. Have some laughter and light-heartedness here. That compassion for yourself will serve you well.

I was mentoring one of my clients who was already a well-established healer. They had lots of training and certificates to their name and had been practicing for years. And yet they just struggled to have a thriving practice. Does this sound familiar?

Many business coaches will tell you to up your prices. Simply charge more and you can make more. How do you feel when you read that? What's your reaction?

Hot tip: *Take 60 seconds to write down all the ways you feel about charging for your service or product. All the good things and all the challenges. Everything is welcome here.*

If you have a product you are selling, this becomes a hard costs issue. How much does it cost to make, transport, package, display and then what is the cost to sell it to your client? Do you have a store? Do you have staff? This becomes a fairly simple formula. Now add your profit. How's the number? Evaluate what you are currently offering and see if you are making any money. Do you like where you are sitting? Does this feel sustainable? Can you offer your product and have a lovely life?

If you are selling your time, this is where a lot of holistic entrepreneurs get tripped up. I have mentored hundreds of holistic entrepreneurs and they struggle to find this sweet spot.

We need to wrap our heads around being in service and what that means to our clients. We also need to wrap our heads around the old, ancient, resonance that when we lived communally, we exchanged services, gifts, food or other items for the gift of healing.

Remember, we are basically still running these old cellular teachings from thousands of years ago. Our bodies are slow to change. Remember the cave lion story? Run east? As healers, we are programmed to see the wellness of the community and prioritize that. We all deserve healing. We all deserve wellness. So how will you rationalize this for yourself in a monetary world?

There are a number of options.

- You could create a barter system;
- You can offer a sliding scale;
- You could offer scholarships;
- You could set your prices quite low and only up them every two or three years;
- You could have evergreen pricing, rewarding clients who come in early with the best price and no rise in what you are charging them over the years;
- You could charge what you're worth (priceless, I know);
- You can offer "pay what you can" days;
- You can offer great packages with reduced rates;

- You can offer payment plans;
- Offer free Matriarch Classes (master classes);
- Do a challenge or summit launch. People can still learn something even if they don't buy from you;
- Have a free Facebook group where you offer great information;
- You can make a "pay it forward" program where someone pays for another client to get a session;
- Occasionally offer discounts or coupons;
- Offer great tips in your newsletter;

Or a combination of any of these systems.

What's important is that you run this idea through your business spreadsheet first, to make sure you can afford it. Did you read that quickly and just keep going? Stop and please read it again. What's important is that you make sure you can afford it, then you can see where you might have wiggle room to offer something differently. For example, I have a formula of, for every 10 people that sign up to my courses, I offer 1 scholarship spot (at a 50% off rate). This is my 10% formula and allows me to know I am making my teachings available to people who might otherwise not be able to afford it. I also offer scholarships, without any need to qualify, to people who are Black, Indigenous or identify as a person of colour. This is an important value for me to ensure people who have been traditionally marginalized have the opportunities to create and sustain the life of their dreams. I have found many ways to share my courses and work with people I want to serve and do it in line with my integrity.

HOT TIP: *This is a really good time for you to evaluate for yourself how much you value anything that is given to you for free. Do you put the time and effort in? Do you value it? Do you think it might not be worth as much because you did not pay for it?*

Many times, as holistic entrepreneurs, especially as we are just starting on this journey, we will want to offer things for free or very low cost. Be careful here. Human nature is to not value things that we do not pay for. Energetically we are setting ourselves up to lower our value in the eyes of our clients, our community and ourselves. Have you heard the phrase "When you pay, you pay attention?"

Do some market research for your business:

- What's the going rate for a similar product or service in your area? If it's $100 (on average) then really feel into that.
- Is that enough?
- Do people charging that have overhead?
- If you come in and charge $40 for that same product or service, what does that do to your industry?

There are no cut and dry answers here, but I do want you to really evaluate how you want to set yourself up within your community.

It's also important to consider if you are putting your clients in an energetic debt. Money is just energy. That's all it is. I exchange this for that. We exchange our time every day for crap and garbage. It could be scrolling mindlessly on your phone, it could be watching TV for hours on end. We are trading our time for something that may not add a lot of value to our lives. Until you can really wrap your brain around this concept "money is just energy" you will have some struggles here, and you might see those struggles reflected back to you from your client's behaviours.

I have no interest in how much money you want to make or how rich you want to be. That is irrelevant to this conversation. As a holistic entrepreneur, you not only need the energy (money) to sustain your life, you also have a responsibility to ensure you are not putting your clients in debt (energetically) either.

I will give you an example of what I mean. I used to offer a "pay what you can" month every February. If you wanted to come and see me for healing, you could bring a card, donation, art from your kid, a book, or cooking. The sky was the limit. Why did I do that? It was important to me to offer up this healing space to others in a way they could access it. Itwas giving back to my community. But why is it "pay what you can?" I need my clients to put some time and energy into it too. I am giving 100%. They need to also.

That keeps the exchange clean. I don't want them feeling indebted to me. I don't want them feeling like they got a handout. I want them to feel empowered and respected and honoured in this space. I need to hold that space out for them. I have something to offer and so do they.

There is another important conversation to have around this concept of energetic debt. When we offer up healing to others at a cost to us, you may find that those clients are difficult, expect more and will cross boundaries. They complain and often feel like what they get is never enough. This is an entitlement mindset on behalf of your client. And yes, we have all experienced moments of entitlement. However, if you are reinforcing this energy pattern with your clients, you are actually reinforcing the victim archetype. Remember the teachings in the Money Archetypes chapter about victim? This is a 2nd chakra issue. As a healer, you have a responsibility to not keep your client's dependant on you or to be enabling them. Think about how an energy deficit might be affecting your business.

Hot Tip: *Reflect back on a relationship that you recognize now may have had an energy deficit. What was going on? What were some of the pain points? How did it make you feel?*

Now, every year when I offer "Pay What You Can", there is a funny hiccup. I can always count on it. Someone will cancel last minute. Always. As in, I won't be able to fill the spot (usually) because it will be in the middle of the day. I have a 48-hour cancellation policy, but when clients haven't paid up front for their appointment, they don't mind sending me an email 10 minutes before their scheduled appointment.

Now, one step further. I had a client book in for "pay what you can". She realized, last minute, that she couldn't make it. She sent me an apologetic note and then e-transferred me money. In fact, she sent me more money that I was currently charging for a 1-hour session. Why? She knew the energetic debt for me and for the community. It was one way to show up.

I can't offer my services to my clients and keep it a fair exchange if I cannot pay the mortgage or put food on the table. I can't offer my services to my clients at a deficit to myself. This is a huge mistake that many entrepreneurs make, and it will sink your business. You are not doing this as a hobby. Your business needs to be sustainable for you to be putting this much energy into it.

Don't place yourself in the saviour or martyr position. Get obvious with yourself about your relationship with money and what you're offering. Realize the power you have to subsidise other clients when you charge appropriately. And remember, if your client can't pay you, they might not be the right client for you.

Finally, get a good bookkeeper. So many entrepreneurs don't understand balance sheets, taxes, and accounting principles. If you can only afford one expert, it should probably be a bookkeeper. Take the time to hire someone who can help you understand your business metrics and the financial aspects. You don't need an accounting or tax degree. Hire someone who can support you and keep you out of hot water, so you can focus on the business of delivering your kick ass product or service.

14

LET'S DO THIS!

Holistic entrepreneurship is a different way of being in the world. Sharing your gifts and services is powerful and needed. Are you willing to put in the work to get your offers out there? Are you willing to deeply prioritize your health, wellbeing and happiness? Are you ready to embrace the student mindset so you can always learn and grow and develop?

Hot Tip: *Review this book and consider:*

- *What chapters have left you a little confused?*
- *What landed really well and made so much sense?*
- *What are the next steps that you can take right now to get you moving in the right direction?*
- *What have you identified as a knowledge gap and need to*

find more information about?

These answers are going to change and evolve as your business does. Take the time to sit with yourself. Evaluate where you are and where you are going. Make your learning and wellbeing a priority and see how that supports you, your family and your business.

I trust that you realized that the one of the most powerful tools at your disposal is your own relationship with yourself. What is your self-talk? What beliefs are holding you back? How do you sabotage yourself? Every single entrepreneur I have ever worked with was able to have the breakthrough and success they wanted because they worked on themselves. That's why this book is so focused on your own wellbeing and mindset.

You not only have the gifts and solutions that people are looking for, but you also now have the inner knowledge, wisdom and some energetic tools you can integrate into your business in an ethical, honouring and win/win way. You no longer need to scramble and be inferior. You don't need to read 15 business books or go get an MBA. Both of those options might be really important to you; that's great, go for it. However, more importantly, is you have grounded yourself into the ways you want to show up, how you can share your work and execute strategies that are not gross, unethical or harmful to yourself or others.

You will mess up. You will trip up. You will fail. All of these realties do not mean you are a mess or that you are a failure.

What it really means is that you are learning and growing. The difference between success and failure is the willingness to try again.

Things might not work out the way you hoped. Can you create space for the multiverse to show up to you and deliver on your dreams in a way that you couldn't imagine? Can you be spacious enough to not attach to timing? How does it feel when you let go of the need to have a destination and allow yourself to enjoy the ride?

That is the work of a holistic entrepreneur. Hold yourself true to your path and your right timing. Explore your relationship to the ideas of harmlessness and compassion. Seek the win/win or no-go scenarios. When you activate these teachings in your life, you will see new possibilities and opportunities that you may have been missing before. You can have the amazing life that you have always dreamed of.

Finally, commit to coming back to this book. As I was writing it, I was weaving health, wellness, growth, opportunity, wealth, magic, and abundance for you. The more you tune into these teachings, own them and make them alive and vivid in your life, the more you will realize the success and joy you want and deserve. Life might not be perfect, but damn, it will be an amazing ride.

Big WILD love to you all.

Xo

Nadine

EPILOGUE

HONOURABLE OPENING CEREMONY.

Ritual can be a powerful way of working within the medicine space of inspired action. An honourable opening ceremony is a beautiful offering to yourself, your business and your clients.

You may be a well-established business or launching a new venture. Either way, if you read this book, created space for honest reveals about where you are and where you are going, and implemented a few of the recommended techniques, this ceremony is right for you.

What you need:

- Candle
- Feather
- Cup of water
- Stone or plant
- Embodiment Board

- 5 Pieces of paper and a pen

Place your embodiment board on the floor. It is the anchor point of your ritual.

Then place the following items around it.

The feather sits in the east.

The candle sits in the south.

The cup of water sits in the west.

The stone or plant sits in the north.

When you have laid out this altar, put on some quiet music in the background.

Light the candle.

Say a brief prayer, intention or simply state aloud "I am now commencing an Honourable Opening Ceremony".

Sit in quiet contemplation. Gaze at your embodiment board and allow yourself to feel the feelings present here.

Celebrate the ways that you feel those feelings every day. Think about what your wish for the world is, and how your business is offering a solution for this. Hold your vision in your mind's eye. Allow this feeling of completeness and wholeness to be flowing in your mind, in your heart and in your body. Breathe deeply into this space. This is your soul medicine.

EAST.

When you are ready, move your attention to the east. Look at your feather. What colour lives here? What type of bird is it from? East represents the mental archetype and new beginnings.

What new beginnings are you putting into the world? Write down what new beginnings you are bringing in with your business (make it simple), then write down one affirmation that you will work with to remind you of this beautiful offering. Write those things on your piece of paper and place them in the East with the feather.

SOUTH.

Move your awareness to the south. Allow yourself to gaze at the flame of the candle. Let your eyes go soft. Seek any messages or wisdom or knowings from the flicker of the candle. The south is about activation.

What do you want to bring to life in the world with this new business? What is the new way of being that you are creating? Then think about something you can do to manifest this. It should be rooted in something you do every day: drink water, take a shower, conscious breathing when you are worried. Write down your activation and inspired action. Place it under the candle.

WEST.

Move your awareness to the west. Allow yourself to see the clear water in front of you. Notice if there are any ripples or if the water is calm. West is about our emotions and shadows.

What emotion would you like to be a little quieter? What emotion do you want to be in the forefront of your business offering? Write down which emotion needs to be quieter (fear, rage, anger, guilt, shame) and then write down (on the other side of the paper) what emotion your business will bring into the world (love, joy, ease, pleasure, knowing, trust, healing). Place that under the water.

NORTH.

Moving your awareness to the north, gaze at your stone or plant. Take notice of anything beautiful or interesting or unique about your choice. Why did you choose this item? The north is about our ancestors and honouring the physical realities of our lives.

What is something you are bringing forward from your ancestors? What is a gift they have given you that you are now able to share in your business? Write this down on your piece of paper and place it under your stone or plant.

CENTRE.

Focus now on the centre of your circle. Your embodiment board should be there. Take the final piece of paper. Remember the feelings you are embodying. Write down what your definition of success could be for the next 12 months. Include three things:

- A personal commitment (eating well, drinking lots of water, moving your body daily, calling your mother once a month);
- A professional promise (emailing your list once a month, posting on social media once a week);
- A knowledge vow (what do you want to learn over the next 12 months) This could be to read a certain book, take a workshop or learn a new piece of software.

Place this in the centre of your circle.

To close your ceremony, take all your pieces of paper from each direction.

Write down the actions for each one.

East = Affirmation.

South = Daily Actions.

West = Emotion you will embody daily and the emotion you will help be a little quieter daily.

North = The ancestral gift and wisdom you are sharing with the world with this new business offering.

For the centre actions, I want you to write them in your daily calendar. Remind yourself how simple this success is. It can be your google calendar or written in your day timer. Seeing this daily will help you embody your success.

Finally, say a closing statement.

> "I close this ritual with deep love and gratitude that I created this time to honour the gifts my business will bring to the world. I am grateful to myself, so many people who have supported me, and the joy and learning this business will offer me. I am so grateful for all the wonderful people I get to serve. I surrender to the medicine of my soul and allow it to guide me. I trust myself, my right timing and know that with inspired action and embodied feelings, I am always successful."

Blow your candle out. Tidy up.

You may wish to sit for a moment and see how you feel. Happy. Scared. Grounded. Grateful. A mixture.

Trust all your feelings and allow all of this to flow with you. Everything you have experienced and learned has brought you here today. You have something special that is needed. Trust your process.

That is a very simple ceremony that allows you to tap into the beautiful offering that your business is. Thank you for showing up in this space and doing this incredible work. You are needed. You are potent. You are loved.

Xo

Nadine

NOTES

4. Your Biggest Asset

1. Archetype: In Jungian psychology, an inherited pattern of thought or symbolic imagery derived from past collective experience and present in the individual unconscious.

   From The American Heritage® Dictionary of the English Language, 5th Edition. Accessed April 8, 2021

10. Imposter Syndrome

1. " Impostor syndrome is a psychological pattern in which an individual doubts their skills, talents or accomplishments and has a persistent internalized fear of being exposed as a "fraud". Despite external evidence of their competence, those experiencing this phenomenon remain convinced that they are frauds, and do not deserve all they have achieved." **Wikipedia** (Accessed Dec 11, 2020)

11. Mentorship and The Perpetual Student

1. "Confirmation bias is the tendency to search for, interpret, favor, and recall information in a way that confirms or supports one's prior beliefs or values. People tend to unconsciously select information that supports their views but ignoring non-supportive information." **Wikipedia**

ABOUT THE AUTHOR

Nadine was a midwife for almost 20 years. After a wild and hairy burnout, she had to repurpose her skills and opened her wellness practice. Nadine thrives when she is mentoring and inspiring people to live the life of their dreams through healing deep soul wounds and helping fierce women get out of their own way.

She is an expert in holistic women's health, a sought after speaker, Creatrix of the Wild Medicine Healer's Training program and an exceptional mentor and healer. She has been a serial entrepreneur her whole life. Nadine has been blissfully partnered with her husband, Michael, for almost 20 years and is a proud mother and grandmother.

You can reach Nadine and find out more at:

www.wildmedicinewoman.ca

Follow Nadine's work here:

facebook.com/peacehealingcalgary
instagram.com/peacehealingwellness

Manufactured by Amazon.ca
Bolton, ON

21938725R00120